GET COURAGEOUS NOW

A WOMAN'S GUIDE TO FINDING HER PASSIONS AND PURPOSE IN LIFE

BY DR. KIKI RAMSEY

Get Courageous Now

Copyright © 2024 by Dr. Kiki Ramsey

Second Edition

KRI Publishing

Second Edition

ISBN- 979-8-218-38442-5

Printed in the USA

Dedication

This Second Edition is still dedicated to my later mother, Alberta Turner, aka "Lucy." Because of you, thousands of women have been motivated by our story, and for that, I am forever grateful.

CONTENTS

ACKNOWLEDGMENTS

I couldn't write a second edition of this book without thanking all the same people I thanked in the first edition.

I thank my husband, Jamil, for your consistent push and enduring love. I'm so blessed that you are my person.

To my fantastic son and twin, Tomazye' the lessons you have taught me about life have been priceless. I love you more than words can say.

To the newest editions to the family, Mackenzie, and Walter, becoming your mother has been one of the biggest desires of my heart. You bring me joy beyond anything I could imagine.

To April, I couldn't have been blessed with a more supportive or loving sister.

To my mother, Lucy, may you continue to rest in Heaven, and I hope I continue to make you proud.

I want to thank all my many wonderful friends and family who continue to encourage and inspire me on this journey I call life.

Lastly, I want to thank all the women who bought this book's first edition and the thousands who will read this second edition. I am eternally grateful for your support.

A PERSONAL NOTE FROM DR. KIKI RAMSEY

The book you hold in your hands is still everything I needed while going through some of my most challenging life experiences and trying to figure out my God-given purpose. I decided to write a second edition because so many things have changed. There is some exciting new research in the field of purpose, meaning, and happiness, and quite frankly, I've changed. I've grown and evolved as a professional, and I have new insights I want to share about being courageous and finding your purpose.

Don't be alarmed because much of the information in the first edition remains the same, but I wanted to provide you with an update in hopes that I can help even more women discover their purpose and passions in life.

So, if you are that women who wants and deserves much more from life than simply existing, this book is for you.

This book is for the woman who has been silently suffering from depression and doesn't know who to turn to; for the woman who appears to be so successful on the outside but is suffering on the inside with so much hurt, so much pain; for the woman who takes care of everyone but herself and feels guilty just taking a little time to relax; for the woman who wants to travel but can't find the time or money to book a vacation once a year; for the woman who has big dreams and passions but can't figure out where to start to accomplish them.

This book is for the woman who has gained weight and wants so badly to lose it all but doesn't have the motivation; for the woman who needs to build financial stability but can't find a way to increase her income; for the woman who wants girlfriends but does not know how to connect with other women.

This book is for the single mother who is struggling to support her family financially and emotionally; for the mother with young children who, on some days, is so stressed out she feels like a bad parent; for the woman with a disabled child who finds it difficult some days to deal with the fact that her child needs so much time and energy; for the woman who is sitting in a jail cell while other people raise her children and regrets the day she ever laid eyes on the place she now calls home.

This book is also for the widow who has lost her husband and is trying to move on with life but can't seem to find the way; for the daughter who has lost her mother and cries every day at the mere thought of living without her; for the woman who is dealing with a parent who has a drug or alcohol addiction and can't figure out why they won't just get help.

This book is for the woman who wants to find love but feels like "the one" is never going to come along; for every wife who is in a bad marriage and can't decide whether to stay or to leave; for every woman who is in or has been in an abusive relationship and needs to know how to pick up the pieces from this tragic connection.

This book is for every woman who knows she was made for a purpose and is ready to get courageous and discover the life she was meant to live.

I want you to know you were made for a purpose, and it's your job to figure out what that is and share it with the world. You can overcome any obstacle and make all your dreams come true. I am so excited to experience your journey of exploration and transformation together. Life is what you make it, and I'm happy you have decided to Get Courageous Now!

Love,

Dr. Kiki

PART I

YOUR FEAR AND YOUR COURAGE

Hey Friend! I am so excited and proud that you decided to pick up and read this book! Making the decision to work towards tackling your fears and becoming courageous is the first step to living your best and most fulfilling life possible.

Let me start off by saying this; we all have situations that cause us to experience immense fear. These situations have a way of knocking us down and keeping us stuck for years. No matter how big, successful or strong you are, you will face some fears in your lifetime. The question is, what will you do when they arrive? You have to look fear in the face and walk right through it. That's the recipe for success. Throughout this book I'm going to teach you how to build unstoppable courage and overcome your fears.

First, however, we're going to explore the concepts of fear, courage, and purpose. You'll learn about your potential for courage and living a purposeful, passionate life, and you'll take a look at the fears that are keeping you from reaching your dreams. The more you know and understand your fears, the easier it will be to work through them later on in your courageous process.

Each chapter of this book has a Courageous Action section where you get to apply what you've learned to your own life. By answering the questions and doing the activities you will have the opportunity to work through your fears. For these sections, set aside a special place to write, like a notebook, journal, or even a digital document you can edit and save. This will be your journal to use on your courageous journey. Keep your journal in a safe place that's easy to reach. It will be a great resource for you while you read the book and a great reference after you have finished.

Are you ready to begin your journey? Here we go!

CHAPTER 1:
THE COURAGE WITHIN YOU

It was 3:00 a.m., and my mom entered my room shouting, "Get up, Kisha, get up!" I jumped up out of bed like the house was on fire. I said, "What's wrong?" She said, "Just get dressed and help your sister get dressed because we have got to go now." I did as I was told, but by then, my sister was crying. I was ten years old, and she was five, and neither of us knew what was going on.

We got our clothes on and all three of us rushed out of the house down a dark lonely road in my neighborhood. My neighborhood was one of those places where you definitely did not want to be out after dark, but there we were, three vulnerable females making our way down the pitch-black streets.

When we arrived at our destination I was told to sit on the couch and not move. I watched my mother disappear up a flight of stairs. There was a clock on the wall in front of me and I watched the hands go by hour after hour. The next thing I knew it was morning and I had fallen asleep right there on that couch. My mom came downstairs and told me and my sister to get our things because we were going home. I wanted desperately to ask her what was going on but she had one of those "don't ask me any questions" looks in her eyes, so I kept quiet.

Life seemed to return to normal. We were back in school having fun and we never spoke about that situation – that is, until it happened again and again and again. I was no stupid little girl and I knew that this was unusual behavior even for my mother. I knew that other kids in my class didn't have to get up at strange hours of the night and go sleep on the couch at someone else's apartment. I started putting clues together and then one day I finally figured it out. I realized that my mother was harboring a secret that would forever change my life. My mother was addicted to crack cocaine, and all those late night runs and sneaking around were for her to get high. That apartment that I slept in night after night was the local crack house. The day I found this out I came to the realization that my life would never be the same again, but I didn't know the worst was yet to come.

Have you ever been at a place in your life where fear has gotten the best of you and you don't know what to do? This was one of those times for me. I didn't know what was going to happen or how my life was going to turn out. I was only ten years old, but I knew I didn't want to be that kid who had to sleep on the couch in a crack house; even more than that I didn't want to be that kid with a mother who was addicted to crack cocaine. But in reality, I was that kid, the one everybody teased about having a crack head for a mother. This was my life and I soon found out that if I had any chance in the world to make it, I was going to have to fight like hell to get there. I was going to have to face some of my toughest fears because nothing else would save me.

This might also be your story. You might be facing one of your toughest challenges yet, such as a difficult financial set-back, the loss of someone you love, or the loss of a job that provided for you and your family. Whatever the challenge might be I understand how it feels to be running very low on hope and solutions. But there is hope! The most important thing I learned during my tough times is you have to dig deep and never give up. I could have given up and who knows, I could have become a crack head myself, but I knew that was not the life God meant for me to live. I knew I had to fight back.

One day I was sitting on that couch in the crack house, mad at the world and even more mad at my mother. I hated the life I was living, a disgraceful type of life that made me want to hide from the world. As I was sitting there thinking about how terrible my life was, something happened inside of me. I began thinking about my future and how it could turn out if I got out of that mess. I remembered what my teacher in school had told me. She said that I could be anything I wanted to be in life, and that I could be successful. When I heard her say those things to me, I began to dream about the possibilities for my life, and it felt good, unlike anything I was currently experiencing. This teacher had no clue about my situation at home but her words resonated with me. I wanted so badly to be successful when I grew up. I wanted not to be sleeping on that couch anymore, and for my mother to stop using drugs. Then it happened – while sitting on that very couch I made a declaration. I promised myself no matter what bad things happened in my life I was going to be successful, period, end of story! My teacher's words gave me the courage to believe that my life could be different than it was. In that moment I got my first glimpse at courage.

That single, simple moment was a turning point in my life. Making the decision at ten years old to be successful no matter what obstacles came my way gave me the strength I needed to overcome my fears and become the woman I am today. For years I fought through challenge after challenge to become the best positive psychologist and executive coach I could possibly be. I wouldn't be here writing to you now if that little seed had not been planted all those years ago.

Before you begin your own courageous process, you need to make a similar promise to yourself. In order to overcome your fear and live your true purpose in life, you need to be willing to take on whatever challenges may appear and find the strength to overcome them and succeed. It won't always be easy, but I promise you that if you put the work in to help your courage grow it will be completely worth it.

You Have the Potential for Courage

So what is courage? To summarize many dictionary entries in my own words, courage is the thing inside you that makes you brave. It's your ability to confront fear, to look fear right in the face and walk through it. The greatest thing about courage is you don't have to be born with it. In fact I don't think that any of us are born with courage; it's something we learn along the way. I believe that with practice anyone can learn to be courageous.

Every human being has the potential to be courageous and much of the time it must be cultivated. The more you use it, the stronger it gets, just like a muscle. You might know people who seem more courageous than others, but that's because life's circumstances may have allowed them to build their courage muscle a little more. For example, I am very proud of my accomplishments, but I did not get where I am today without building my courage. It was a process; it didn't happen all at once.

If you have trouble imagining yourself as a courageous person, think back to what you were like in your early childhood. Many of us had almost limitless courage when we were little, because we hadn't yet been "taught" by our circumstances to be afraid. As I was growing up I was what some might call a little daredevil. I would run and jump in and out of trees and I was never scared of the consequences. One morning at the bus stop everyone dared me to race against one of the fastest boys in my neighborhood. Let's think logically about this. First of all I was a girl and he was a boy and many people think boys are faster.

Secondly we were in front of the whole neighborhood which meant everyone could see my defeat if I lost. The kids in my neighborhood were pretty rough and if I lost I was sure to hear about it for a long time. But even knowing all of this I decided to take on this challenge.

I went to the starting line and took a deep breath. When I heard the word "Go!" I ran with all my might! And guess what? The race ended in a tie! Can you believe that? My courage and adrenaline allowed me to push through to the finish line and, most importantly, kept me from losing in front of the entire neighborhood. Courage was alive and well in my life at this time but as the years went on it began to dwindle more than I wanted it to.

There have been periods in my life when I wondered where my courage had gone. During these times I had become way too comfortable with my mediocre life. I didn't know how to face tough challenges, and I started to care way too much about what people thought of me. Unfortunately, this happens to a lot of us. As children, we are courageous, but as adults, our courage seems to vanish into thin air. The good news is it's not gone for good, and you can build your courage over and over again. The secret is to practice. You must use your courage muscle on a continuous basis. When a scary situation presents itself, it's your opportunity to practice. The more you practice the better you will get at overcoming your fears.

I invite you now to go on a courageous journey with me. On this journey, you will learn how to navigate your fears, and along the way, you will become more and more courageous. Rest assured that you can and will get past any challenge that you are currently facing and in the end you will be able to wholeheartedly say that you have created a happy, purposeful life.

Courageous Action Step:

A. Answer these questions in your journal:

- When did fear first show up in your life?

- Were you courageous as a child? If so what were some of the times when you showed courage?

- How courageous do you feel right now on a scale of 1 to 10? (10 being the most courageous and 1 being the least courageous)

B. Are you ready to tackle your challenges and build your courage? Make a promise to yourself that you are going to be successful in your life, no matter what! You can write your promise in your journal, say it out loud to yourself, or even put the words somewhere you can see them every day – whatever will help you most on your journey to get courageous and create meaningful change in your life.

Here's an example of a promise, but go ahead and use your own words if you like:

"I promise to do everything humanly possible to overcome my obstacles and fear. I know I have what it takes to overcome anything that comes my way. I know I have so much courage built up just waiting to come out. I promise to unleash my courage so I can have the life I deserve."

Courageous Lessons Learned:

Everybody has the potential for courage. You don't have to be born with courage; you can learn to be courageous. The more you practice and use your courage muscle, the more it grows.

CHAPTER 2:
YOU WERE MADE FOR A PURPOSE

Maybe you picked up this book because you liked the new and updated cover. Thank you design team. But most likely you picked it up because the title spoke to you. In that case chances are you feel that you have been made for so much more and there has to be more to life. The good news is you're right, and you are about to find out why.

Now that you know about your potential for courage, we are going to talk about one of my favorite things in the world – purpose. The truth is you're going to need courage to pursue your purpose. So what is purpose? Purpose is the real reason you exist. It's the one thing you were placed on earth to do, and when you are walking in your purpose it makes life so much better. I believe God placed everyone on this earth for a certain assignment and it's your job to find out what that assignment is. In my work with women I've found that some women know their purpose, but many more only have a vague idea about their purpose or don't know their purpose at all. Regardless of where you are on the spectrum you must first know that you were made for a purpose.

The reason I am so passionate about teaching you to be courageous enough to walk through your fears is because I know that on the other side of your fears lies your purpose in life. If you are brave enough to set your fears aside and push through you will discover your true calling in life.

Let me give you an example. When I was sixteen years old, I got pregnant, and at seventeen, I gave birth to my son Tomazye'. During this time I thought my life was over. I truly thought that there was no hope for me and that my future didn't exist. Then one day I got a call from the Greenville Council for Prevention of Teen Pregnancy. They had heard about how much I loved to talk and how energetic I was. They thought I would be a good candidate to go around to all the other high schools in the county and teach other teens about preventing teen pregnancy. Go figure. I was super shocked but of course I took the job. In return they agreed to pay for my son's daycare as long as I didn't have another child. After all their whole goal was to prevent teen pregnancy.

I started going around to all the high schools and talking to the students about why they shouldn't get pregnant at such a young age. This was my first real speaking job, but at the time I didn't realize it. Sharing my story with other teens sparked my love for speaking. As the years went on I realized that speaking and pouring positivity into others was my true gift and I needed to use it to help people. Now, if I had continued to wallow in my embarrassment about getting pregnant at a young age, or if I had listened to all the people who doubted my ability to make a better life for myself, I would never have taken on the challenge of standing up in front of a class full of my peers and saying "Don't be like me, be better than me." My purpose was born out of my pain and today I am able to stand up in front of thousands of women just like you and say, "You can do and become anything you want no matter what you have been through."

As I've thought about and researched the topic of purpose I came up with my own acronym for the word, and all in all I think it describes purpose to a T:

Proclaim the promise of God in your life. A lot of times we hold back what we are feeling or dreaming about because we are scared to profess it to the world for fear of judgment. However, I truly believe that our purposes in life are God-given. It says in Jeremiah 29:11, "For I know the plans I have for you, plans to prosper you and not to harm you. Plans to give you a future and a hope." If God Himself has given you a purpose in life, surely you can be courageous enough to proclaim with joy and confidence that He has big things planned for you. Be brave, open up your mouth, and tell the world your passions and dreams.

Unlock the dreams inside you. It's time to dig deep and discover the dream that's inside of you. I know it's there. Most of us have dreams, but we're too scared to unlock them for fear of what might happen. Put your fear aside and take the padlock off so you can discover your destiny.

Recognize that you were made for greatness. Greatness is in each of us, but so often women play small. You have the ability to be and do anything you want in this lifetime, but only if you believe it and are willing to do what it takes to make it happen. Don't be discouraged by the challenges that come your way. Great people are born by overcoming great challenges and doing great things.

Pursue your passions. A lot of women downplay what they are passionate about. Knowing what your passions are is a big deal, because they are the gateway to your purpose. When you are truly passionate about something you are willing to give the time and energy needed to cultivate that passion into something amazing. Discovering your passions and pursuing them will be one of the most rewarding things you ever do.

Overcome whatever challenges come your way. You are going to have to face challenges – it's a fact. Your challenges will look and feel different from anyone else's and get ready because they are coming. The best thing to do is anticipate that you're going to face challenges at some point on your journey and prepare yourself to weather the storm. You have to conquer a challenge to reach success.

Serve the world with your gifts. Everyone was placed on earth with at least one gift. It is your job to use your gift(s) for the benefit of others as often as you can. The world needs what you have to give. You are unique, and no one can serve the world quite like you can.

Embrace the life you were meant to live. You were meant to live an amazingly good, happy and healthy life and it's time you embrace this fact. Life is totally what you make it. There are so many wonderful experiences to be had. It's time to live, laugh and love.

So there you have it, my definition of purpose broken down. You can use this as a reference as you go through this book. I hope it inspires you to really dig deep to discover and live out your purpose.

Your Passion

I mentioned passion in my acronym, but I want to go into more detail because passion is such an important part of discovering and living out your purpose. Passion is the drive inside of you that makes you want to move forward in your life with the things you love, or that makes you want to fight against the things that cause you or others you care about to feel pain. It's that emotion you feel when you can't wait to do something, or when you can't stand to see something or someone go through an experience that is unnecessary. Even when things get tough, passion shines through. As you have already experienced, life can get very tough, but when you are truly passionate about something you are willing to keep going against all odds.

Let's say you are like me and you are passionate about helping poor women and children in disadvantaged countries get the supplies they need to survive. Every year you would raise $3000 through generous donors to go to your chosen country to provide food, water, school supplies and a lot of love. You got to know those women and children personally by name and you couldn't imagine not going. Now let's say you fell on hard times financially and you could no longer go to your country. Your generous donors were not giving like they were in the past. If you were as passionate as I am about helping the women and children in your country you would find a way to get there because those people mean everything to you. In my case when I first started missionary work and didn't have much money I pushed hard to raise all the money I needed, even taking large portions of my own money to make sure I made it to Kenya six years in a row. This is all because I am truly passionate about the women and children of that country. Being willing to persist in the face of hard times is the true definition of passion.

Being passionate is one of the most important factors in determining your purpose in life, because when you are deeply passionate about something it becomes your purpose. It becomes your mission in life, what you were placed here on earth to do.

Some people get a little confused when talking about purpose because it seems to them like anyone could do what it is they are purposed for. If I think about it, yes, anyone can speak to a crowd of women and empower them to transform their life and career; many people do that very same thing right now. And yes, many people can go to Kenya and provide love, support and food to the women and children there; all of my fellow missionaries are great at it. The difference is no one can do it the way I can. And no one can do what you were meant to do like you can. I firmly believe that God has specific assignments He wants us to do and specific people He wants us to affect through our purpose. If we don't step up to the call then we miss our assignment and the blessing He was trying to provide to someone else through us. When we don't step into the fullness of our purpose we miss opportunities that were meant only for us.

When you answer your calling to your purpose the world opens up to you and opportunities that you would have never imagined possible present themselves. Why does this happen? Well, have you ever heard the saying, "When the student is ready the teacher appears"? When you are ready for a life change you will begin to understand that there is always a way to make it happen. In the end it doesn't matter what your challenges in life are because purpose always wins out. Remember, where there is passion there is purpose, and where there is purpose there is a lifetime of happiness.

Unfortunately, your fears can often be a powerful enemy to your passions and purpose, holding you back from your best life. In the next few chapters we are going to take a look at how fear is affecting your life before we begin our courageous journey to take fear head-on.

Courageous Action Step:

A. Your passion and your purpose go hand in hand. When you discover your purpose, you will usually find it's something you are truly passionate about.

It's time to clear your mind and answer a series of passion- and purpose-driven questions. Write your responses down in your journal. These may be some of the most important questions you will ever answer.

Passion-Driven Questions:

1. What new things do you want to try?

2. When you were younger, what did you want to be when you grew up? What activities did you like back then?

3. What activities do you like to do now?

4. What makes you smile?

5. What makes you get excited?

6. What things do you secretly like, but haven't told anyone that you like?

7. What places do you want to travel to?

Purpose-Driven Questions:

1. What are you great at? What are your strengths?

2. What hurts? What bothers you when you see it or hear about it?

3. What makes you cry? What makes you angry?

4. What things do you value and why?

5. Who do you admire and what qualities do you like about them?

6. What would you do for a living if you did not have to worry about money?

7. What cause are you willing to fight for?

8. What services can you provide to make someone's life and the world a better place?

B. As a Positive Psychologist I tend to look at things from the positive side. Therefore, instead of calling it a Bucket List I have embraced calling it a Life List. Therefore, for this assignment write out your Life List. In your journal, write down 50- 100 things you would like to do while you are still living. Try to get as close to one hundred things as possible. Then narrow your list down to ten of your favorites. After that, narrow your list down again to five of your favorites. Then down to three. By now you should be getting closer to the things that mean the most to you.

Make sure you have easy access to these two exercises so you can come back and look at your answers later.

Courageous Lessons Learned:

You were made for a purpose. Your true passions become your purpose in life. Where there is passion there is purpose, and where there is purpose there is a lifetime of happiness.

CHAPTER 3:
WHAT IS YOUR FEAR FACTOR?

Let's get deep and talk about fear. Fear is the little four letter word that has ruined thousands, even millions of lives. It's absolutely crazy when you think about it. Fear is the emotion that keeps you from reaching your full potential. It's the thing that holds you back even though you know you were meant to do so much more. It keeps you up at night worrying about your overdue bills, your health, and the status of your relationships. All of the negative thoughts that creep into and across your mind stem from fear.

Why is fear so powerful? The answer to this question might surprise you, because although we normally don't think of fear as a good thing, it actually has good intentions. The truth is fear is there to protect you from danger. When something scares you, fear tries to protect you from it. For instance, if a dog were chasing you, fear would kick in and tell you to run. The frustrating thing about fear is that it doesn't have a brain. It can't differentiate between what's dangerous and what's going to help you live a better life, and it doesn't know when it's hindering you from something that's good for you. When you are feeling too scared to step outside of your comfort zone, fear doesn't know that facing a challenge will be beneficial and help you grow; it only knows to kick in and protect you.

Now we have a problem, because fear is always going to do the job it was commissioned to do, which is to keep you safe. Here's the big reveal – since fear does not have the brains to figure out which situations are helpful to you and which are genuinely dangerous, it is your job to tell fear that it needs to go away when it is not the appropriate time or place. I know you might be saying, "Ok Dr. Kiki, I really get what you are saying about fear and all, but how do you make it go away?" I am so happy you asked because we are going to be working together to overcome all your fears throughout this book, but right now I want you to start with taking a fear assessment. I want you to figure out what fear is actually costing you. I call this your Fear Factor. This is just a little equation laid out in terms of money to help you realize what fear may be costing you in actual dollars. In this exercise I use money because it's easy to understand money and most people are looking for ways to increase their income. When you do this exercise, you will truly understand the depth of fear and how it plays a major role in hindering you from accomplishing your goals.

When I first did the Fear Factor equation for myself I was totally shocked because I had been in such denial about my full potential. I didn't know how much I was selling myself short, or that my fears were costing me so much. Deep down I knew I was smart and capable of doing so much more but I was choosing to live my life on a small scale and was afraid to step out of my comfort zone to pursue my dream. My decision to overcome my fears and become a professional speaker has been one of the best choices I have ever made. Over the years I have realized how much I have to offer and now I refuse to sell myself short ever again.

Courageous Action Step:

Calculate Your Fear Factor

A. Answer this question: How much money do you want to make each month? (I love this exercise because everyone can relate to money.) When you are thinking about this number remember that the world absolutely needs your calling. This is not the time to downplay your skills and abilities. It doesn't matter whether you are a stay at home mother, entrepreneur, or corporate executive. I want you to simply write down how much money you want to make each month. Think about your life and how you would enjoy it if you had the money you wanted, needed and deserved. When you get this number write it down in your journal.

B. Now write down how much money you are currently making per month. Write this number beneath the first number. Remember this current income may be from your full-time job, part-time job, or business – whatever money you are making right now to support yourself.

C. Subtract the money that you are currently making from the money that you want to be making. Put a big fat circle around the number that you just came up with. This is your Fear Factor! This is how much fear may be factored into you not making the type of money you want to make in your life.

Example: Let's say you think you should be making $10,000 a month for all the awesome work that you do, but you are only making $4000 a month. The difference between what you should be making and what you are actually making is $6000 a month. This $6000 is your Fear Factor. This number represents what your fear could potentially be costing you every single month in dollars.

Is this number shocking to you? It might be hard to believe that your fear could be costing you this much every month. Your fear has been holding you back so much that you have not been able to reach your full potential and earn the kind of money you deserve or want. When I first did this exercise I was completely blown away by the difference in the two numbers. My fear factor was three times what I was currently making at the time. That meant my fear was certainly holding me back and I needed to do something about it.

D. Let's take it a step further and break this number down even more. Divide your fear factor number by four. This is what your fear is costing you every single week.

In our example fear is costing you $1500 a week.

E. Now divide your fear factor by 30 and this is what your fear is costing you every single day.

In our example fear is costing you $200 a day. This is a lot of money to be missing out on due to fear.

F. Now multiply your fear factor by 12 and this is how much money you could be earning every year if you decided to overcome your fears and realize your full potential!

In our example fear is costing you an additional $72,000 a year! Now that's money I'm sure you could put to good use.

G. This equation is based on money, and is a good indication of how much you are selling yourself short in terms of your salary and finances. You may want to consider other forms of Fear Factor tests and do those in your journal as well:

- Is time more important to you than money? Calculate how many hours each month you want to spend, versus how many you actually spend, on things that are important to you and that you are genuinely passionate about. Do the same calculations for each week and day.

- How many people in your life do you wish you had meaningful, positive relationships with? How many people do you actually have such relationships with?

- How many new things did you want to try in the last year? How many did you actually try?

- How many opportunities that interested you presented themselves to you within the last year? How many did you actively pursue?

So now I ask you, what is fear costing you? Are you shocked by these numbers? You should be. This is what it costs you not to walk in your greatness. This is what fear is costing you not to live every single day to the fullest of your capability.

How much are you selling yourself short? Has your fear factor revealed some shortcomings? I'm sure the answer is yes, but the good news is you can and will tackle your fears. The first step is in the realization. Have faith that you can reach your Fear Factor numbers.

Courageous Lessons Learned:

Your Fear Factor is only a measure of how much your fear has been holding you back. Although the number may be big you have the capacity to reach that number and eliminate your fears.

CHAPTER 4:
THE EIGHT MAIN FEARS THAT HOLD PEOPLE BACK

Now that you realize how much your fears are holding you back, it's time for you to understand that fear shows up in many different forms. As a positive psychologist and executive coach I have researched many fears over the years, and unfortunately I have also experienced most of them. I know for a fact that I have allowed my fears to keep me from living in my purpose in the past. The key is to identify which fears scare you the most, so that when the fear shows up you will recognize it and know what to do about it.

In my research eight of the same fears kept repeating themselves over and over again. I have noticed in all my work with women that any one of these fears can have a huge impact on a woman's life, and most have hindered women from reaching their full potential. It is my job to expose these fears to you so that they will no longer hold you back. As we go through the eight different fears, I want you to pay close attention and identify the ones that have kept you from living your most amazing life.

1. Fear of the Unknown

So many people have trouble with the fear of the unknown. When you have this fear, the mind tells you that in order to move forward you must know what's going to happen, because if you know then you can control the situation and the outcome. We as humans love to feel like we are in control. Control establishes a measurement that we can use to manipulate the results of our actions. We don't like the unknown simply because we don't understand it or have a plan to control it.

When I met my husband Jamil I was pretty much done with men. I had been lied to and cheated on one too many times. I was sick and tired of getting my heart broken. So when my husband showed up on the scene I was very skeptical about him.

First of all we met online. Back then online dating was not as big or researched as it is now. There was a huge unknown factor involved. What if he was a stalker or a murderer? Now don't act like you have never had those thoughts before. However, my deeper fears were, what if he hurts me like all the other men? What if he tells me he loves me and then leaves me? These are the questions that you may have asked yourself as it pertains to your relationship. The truth is none of us really knows what to expect when it comes to meeting someone new. There is a chance that you could meet the man of your dreams and there is a chance that you could meet the man of your nightmares. Either way it's an unknown and if you want a shot at true love you have to give it a chance.

Our first meeting was at a Sonic restaurant. We had been talking on the phone for a while so I felt like I knew him, but just to be on the safe side I thought it would be better to meet him in public in case my stalker or murderer intuition was right. When he arrived I was so happy to finally meet him in person. We hit it off right away and the meeting went really well.

However, I needed to make sure he was legit, so I took him to my church revival and left him with my friend so she could tell me how he behaved when I wasn't around. Yes, I know this might sound a little crazy, but it was my test to see if he was who he said he was and if he loved God like he said he did. I figured he would be freer to be himself if he wasn't trying to impress me. I must say he passed the test and got two thumbs up from my friend. Afterwards we went to a nice restaurant, had a beautiful dinner and talked the night away. After that night we were inseparable and we fell in love. Then the most amazing thing happened – six months later he proposed and I said yes! Now I am certainly glad I didn't control this unknown because I would have never imagined that this online connection would end up being my husband.

Here's my question to you – are you allowing fear of the unknown to hold you back from doing or experiencing something important? If so you need to identify that fear so that you can tackle it.

2. Fear of Failure

The fear of failure rules over all of our actions and decisions. We all do or don't do things in order to avoid failure. This is where most people begin to give themselves excuses not to do a certain task or take the risks that they should be taking. This is when people begin to self-sabotage their efforts because they are too scared to even try.

This fear is very tricky. You see, when you are petrified of failure, messages are sent to your brain that say, "Why do that when you know it's not going to turn out right? Why even try?" When these messages hit your subconscious brain you respond by not trying. You then find yourself with a lack of motivation, energy or power to get started on new projects because you already sent yourself defeating messages. This is a very dangerous fear to live with.

Another message that the fear of failure sends is that you must be perfect or things must be in perfect order for you to move ahead. Perfectionism is a lie, because the truth is nothing can ever be perfect. No one on earth is perfect. But with the fear of failure you tell yourself that if it's not perfect you cannot show it to the world. Just because something isn't perfect doesn't mean it's a failure. Actually failure is a very subjective term because everyone's perspective is different, so what counts as failure to you might not count as failure for another person. You might view getting a C on a paper as a failure but another person might see it as a success. What matters is what you do when you are faced with failure.

Here's the cold hard truth – you will face failure at some point in your life. Yes, I said it, but here's the good part – I believe it's your failures that shape your life, not your successes. The reason I say this is because you must fail before you succeed. If you surveyed some of the most successful people in the world they would tell you that they failed many times before they got it right. I see so many women trying their hardest not to fail, and they are not aware that they are stunting their growth to success. I have realized through my own failures that you learn so many lessons by failing.

I wanted to become a professional speaker for a very long time. For years I tried other businesses thinking they would give me the success I needed in order to consider myself a speaker. Then one day while I was sitting in a business meeting I finally decided that I was going to quit that business and start speaking professionally. I'd had enough of watching others, namely the leaders in my company who were responsible for motivating us during the meetings, live out my dream.

Over time I did my research and I finally booked my very first speech at a local rotary club meeting. On the day of my big speech I was super excited and very nervous. This was going to be my big chance to show the world (or at least the people who showed up that day) that I had the talent to be a professional speaker. I had practiced and I was well prepared for this speech. I had been taught not to use notes when I was doing a keynote speech because you are able to connect with the audience so much better without notes. Therefore I had memorized my speech verbatim and I was ready.

Jamil and I arrived at the club. Jamil has always supported me in everything that I have done, so it was no surprise that he would be front and center for my first professional speech. As I was being introduced I took one last deep breath, glanced at my notes, and went to the center of the floor where I would be speaking – and I froze. I just stood there for what felt like eternity with a very blank stare on my face. For the life of me I could not remember the first word of the first sentence I was supposed to say. At this time in my speaking career I wasn't seasoned enough to just wing it. I needed my notes. So I did the only thing I knew how to do. I told the audience to please excuse me for a minute and I walked over to the table where my husband was sitting along with my notes. I glanced at the first sentence, then resumed my previous position and began my speech. I was so humiliated. I couldn't believe I forgot my first line. I felt like I was the worst speaker in the world. How could I call myself a speaker if I couldn't even remember the first sentence of a speech I had practiced every day for the last month? All I wanted to do was hurry up and get the speech over with before the club kicked me out for doing such a horrible job. In my eyes I had surely failed.

To my surprise, when I was finished the entire audience (all twenty people) clapped for me and gave me a lot of praise. I wanted to ask them if they were talking to the right person, but I didn't. My husband even told me I did very well, and he has never been one to lie to me about my abilities. He is usually honest with me, sometimes a little too honest. Here's the kicker – I was even asked to do another speech at the local community college sometime in the future. That blew my mind. That is what all speakers wish would happen when they speak.

This was such an eye-opening experience for me. I was so afraid to fail at being a professional speaker it took years and a lot of heartache before I would even give it a try. When I did finally give it a shot I still stumbled, but I made it through and it turned out better than I ever imagined. I know now that failure is a part of life and I vow to not let it hinder me ever again. I hope you can learn the same from hearing my example.

3. **Fear of Pain**

We as humans avoid pain and look for pleasure in almost everything we do. It's called the pain and pleasure principle. This principle was created by Sigmund Freud the founder of modern psychotherapy. You actually know this principle very well but maybe you have not heard it explained in simple terms. All humans are born with a pleasure principle, which means we want immediate gratification and we are rewarded with feelings of pleasure when our needs are met. The opposite is also true, and the pain principle says we look to avoid pain by seeking pleasure. In simple terms, if the pleasure of doing something bad for you is more than the pain of quitting then you will continue to do what's bad for you.

Let's take quitting smoking for example. Most smokers associate more pleasure with smoking than they do pain. The pleasure they feel may include soothing relaxation, less stress, etc. These people associate more pain with quitting smoking than they do pleasure. When people quit they begin to get headaches, anxiety, nausea and a craving for more tobacco. The withdrawal from smoking is painful. In this scenario the pain of smoking has not become great enough for the person to stop.

Now for this person to change, they have to attach enough pain to the behavior of smoking that it makes them want to quit. They must also attach enough pleasure to the new behavior of not smoking that it makes them want to move forward in their life smoke-free. The pain of smoking means you might suffer from major health problems such as lung disease or a chronic cough. The pleasure of not smoking means you will have healthy lungs, more energy and quite possibly a better outlook on life.

We all have things that we can associate with the pain and pleasure principle. For me, it shows up in the area of food. I'd rather eat what I want to eat when I want to eat it than eat healthy foods. When I'm fighting this battle, the pain of watching others eat or just not being able to eat what I want kills me. Sometimes I give in to my bad eating habits because the foods that I love are just so darn good. But when I come to my senses and realize that eating those things is damaging to my body and causing me to gain unwanted weight in my belly area, it makes me want to quit eating poorly. When I begin to associate pleasure with not eating those bad things and having a small midsection I eat better. Just knowing this principle and how to deal with it can help you overcome the fear of pain.

4. Fear of Rejection

This social fear is one of the main reasons people act the way they do. We tend to (sometimes blindly) follow others because it helps us avoid dealing with rejection from society. We fear rejection because most of us can only justify our existence through the acknowledgement and acceptance of others.

Now don't get me wrong, I certainly understand wanting to fit in – but what I have experienced and witnessed with my own two eyes is that we get totally wrapped up in what others think of us instead of dealing with our feelings about ourselves. We fear rejection so much that we try to be who we think we're supposed to be, rather than who we really are.

Let me ask you a serious question – are you a people pleaser? If you said yes to this question there are thousands of women who can relate with you, including myself, although right now I consider myself a recovering people pleaser. People like us always want others to be happy and we think it's our job to make them happy. A lot of the time we do this at the expense of our own well-being. It seems like we just don't know how to say no. You understand exactly what I'm talking about if you are a person that has a hard time telling others no even when it puts you at a disadvantage.

Telling someone no used to be one of the hardest things for me to do. My husband would call me and ask me to do something and I would say ok. Then my son would need me to do something for him and I would say yes. Then my sister would call and ask me to do something for her and I would say yes. My friends would want to go out and do something and I would say yes to them too. One week I literally overextended myself so much that on Friday when I came home from work I broke down crying and fell asleep from sheer exhaustion because I had been running my body like crazy for several weeks. I had committed to way too much; my body was tired and it responded accordingly. On top of that I was also emotionally drained.

It was right then and there that I decided that I could no longer live my life being a "yes girl". I had to put a stop to the madness. I wasn't upset with the people I had made commitments to; I was upset with myself because I allowed my life to become so overwhelming. I began to ask myself why I felt the need to say yes to everyone's requests, and the answer was shocking. After thinking over this question I realized that I did not value my time. That's not to say that the people and the things I was spending my time on weren't worthy, but I realized I did not value spending time with myself. Wow, now that's deep! I thought if I had free time in my life I should be doing something with it, and if others asked me for a favor I should honor their request because I had the free time. I always felt like if I said no then people would not like me and they would reject me. I didn't think that spending the free time with myself doing whatever I wanted was beneficial. At that time I was more concerned about what others thought of me, and not my heath.

That Friday night I came home from work and literally slept until the next morning. I had things planned for that night, but I couldn't do anything else for anyone. People were calling and texting me but I couldn't respond. The next morning my husband told me that when he got home I was sound asleep on the bed in my clothes and he didn't want to wake me so he allowed me to sleep. He also fielded my calls and told everyone that I was sleeping. I must say that was some of the best sleep I had gotten in a long time, and when I woke up I realized that my health was more important then others' opinions of me. I knew I had to start doing the work on myself in this area. I had to look deep within and begin to value my time spent with myself. I had to learn to say no.

5. Fear of Loneliness

For the majority of people, having to spend too much time by themselves is a dreaded experience. The fear of being alone, also called monophobia, is a feeling of emptiness caused by the absence of interaction with another human being. Most of the time these feelings of loneliness are mild. You might feel uneasy that your spouse is away on a trip or you might feel sad because you have to go to the movies by yourself. You might be like me and really enjoy human interaction. At other times, however, this fear can really hinder your progress in life and even your personal happiness.

Let's take relationships for example. How many people do you know who are in bad relationships, but refuse to leave? The other person may not show a lot of interest in them or may even be mean, rude, or abusive, and yet they stay anyway. Too many times we get into and stay in relationships not because they're good for us, but because we're afraid of being alone.

I used to date this guy I was super in love with. I thought he was amazing! He was a jock and I loved that about him because I was also an athlete. We would spend lots of time together which was very important to me (and it still is); I literally wanted to spend all my time with him. We would get wrapped up in conversations and next thing you know it would be morning.

Then he started calling less frequently and didn't come around as often. When I asked him about the changes in his behavior he gave me all kinds of excuses, like he had to work late or he had a late class. After a lot of investigation I found out that he was cheating on me. I did break up with him, but after a while I forgave him and we got back together. The funny thing is, he continued to cheat on me and it became a vicious cycle of him cheating, me forgiving and us getting back together. At this time in my life I was so afraid of being alone that I allowed this situation to go on for several years until I'd had enough. I finally had the sense to understand that this man was not going to change and that I would be better off alone than continuously subjecting myself to this treatment.

I ended the relationship once and for all and never looked back after he told me he was out having dinner with his second baby's mother at some fancy restaurant. He told me she needed to eat because she was carrying his child, which shocked me because I was unaware that he had another child on the way. Right then I just couldn't take it anymore and I had to trust that being alone couldn't feel as bad as this. Fortunately, I realized that being alone was going to be better than staying in that relationship.

What's interesting is that according to research, 60 percent of married people feel lonely in their relationship. This could stem from feelings of disconnectedness or a lack of true intimacy.

The fact remains that 40 percent of us will feel some type of loneliness at some point in our lives and you need to be on the lookout if this is your fear.

6. Fear of Inadequacy

Inadequacy is all about the standards and expectations we set for ourselves. Some of us have very high standards and we're our own worst critics. The truth is other people might not expect as much of us as we do of ourselves, but we project our feelings of inadequacy onto the world and in turn it makes us feel horrible when we don't live up to those "norms" or standards. Now don't get me wrong, everyone feels inadequate about their shortcomings at some point, but it becomes a problem when we allow this fear of inadequacy to hinder our progress in life.

When I decided to start my professional speaking business I felt inadequate about my skills. I questioned myself all the time. Was I good enough to speak in the corporate world? Was I good enough to speak in front of large audiences? What if I messed up in front of everyone? These were just some of the thoughts that ran through my head on a regular basis. The funny thing is I had no evidence as to why I was asking these questions. I was actually really good at speaking in front of an audience, and if I did mess up (which I did on occasion), no one would ever know. In order to overcome this fear I had to tell myself to keep going no matter how I felt, and that's exactly what I did. Because I proceeded with my goal of speaking to as many audiences as I could, my fear of inadequacy in this area of my life soon subsided. I still get nervous every time I speak, not because I feel inadequate but because I want to go out and do my very best for my audience. But over the years I have learned to turn my nervousness into excitement every time I step onto that stage.

7. Fear of Lack

When we talk about lack, you might think of the word poverty. Poverty is defined as a situation that comes from the lack of the resources needed to completely fulfill our human needs. These may include basic food, shelter and clothing, but in reality, some of us have a fear of lacking the things that we perceive will make us happy such as a nice house, a nice car or even enough money to do the things we want to do when we want to do them like getting our hair and nails done. Therefore the fear of lack is sometimes exacerbated by true poverty and other times exacerbated by our own wants. In any case this can be a tough fear, because feeling like you don't have enough or actually not having enough can be super scary.

I've talked to so many women who stay in a job they hate just because they have the security of knowing that their bills are going to get paid at the end of the month. These women are trying to avoid their fear of lack, but they are missing out on a potentially rewarding career somewhere else.

When I was a child my family had a lot of money problems. We lived in the projects, a very bad neighborhood, and my mother always worked very labor-intensive jobs with low pay. I remember being on welfare and food stamps and hating it. We never had enough of the things I wanted such as shoes and clothes. We even had a few touch and go times when we lost our apartment and we had to go stay with family and friends. This type of living made it really hard for me to handle money as an adult. Before I learned to overcome my fear of lack I was always very nervous about not having enough money, and in many cases as an adult I didn't have enough money to buy the things I wanted which really hindered my financial progress. However, as I began to understand money and the hold it had over me I was able to break free. Now I am so much better at handling my money than I ever thought possible, and I also learned to put certain things in place, such as saving, so I wouldn't have to worry about a lack of money.

8. Fear of Success

Success can be awesome but it can also be very scary for some people. There is a lot of work that goes into becoming successful and it often takes great effort and a lot of hard work. It is easier to stay in your comfort zone than to reach new goals, or to open yourself up for people to criticize and watch you. Women are often afraid of success because they fear if they become too powerful they will become unlovable, which ties in to the fear of loneliness. People also fear success because it brings them into the public eye, which means others will start pointing fingers and talking about them. Success can even lead to changes in friends and the people around you, which is frightening for many people.

I have known I would be successful from the moment I made myself that promise while sitting on that couch, but knowing and actually going after success are two different things. Several years before starting my Get Courageous seminar I went to my event planner and told her that this was going to be the year that I actually launched the seminar. After going through some details on what it would take for Get Courageous to be successful, including the financial numbers, I decided not to go forward with it. Thoughts of failure certainly were going through my head, but so were thoughts of success. What if I succeeded? What if Get Courageous was a major success? How many women would I have to host? How difficult would it be to please and help hundreds of women? After going back and forth with my planner for several years I finally decided to embrace success and launch Get Courageous despite my fears. I'm happy to say that was in 2012 and while I was hosting Get Courageous it changed hundreds of women's lives.

Now that you've learned about the eight biggest fears that hinder people from achieving their purpose in life and living their dreams, you may be thinking about how these fears affect your own life. It may seem overwhelming at first to go up against such major obstacles, but don't worry. Throughout the rest of the book, I'll guide you through confronting and overcoming each one of these fears to live in your passions and purpose.

Courageous Action Step:

Answer these questions in your journal:

1. Which one of these eight fears resonated with you the most and why?

2. What is your biggest fear in life? (Use the above as a guide. Once you identify your biggest fear you will have something to target working on throughout this book.)

Courageous Lessons Learned:

There are eight main fears that tend to hold most people back from reaching their full potential: fear of the unknown, fear of failure, fear of pain, fear of rejection, fear of loneliness, fear of inadequacy, fear of lack, and fear of success. You don't have to let these fears keep you from living a life full of purpose and joy. You can overcome each one.

PART II:

THE SEVEN STEP COURAGEOUS PROCESS

In the previous chapters you became familiar with your fears. You now know what fear is costing you and which fears hinder you the most. Now it's time to learn the process that will help you be courageous enough to face and overcome your fears and discover your purpose in life.

For every challenge that you face you must do the work to overcome it. I wholeheartedly believe that if you are unable or unwilling to do the work you may as well stop reading this book right now. I am giving you a little bit of tough love here, but I only want you to become all that you want to be. If you know that you are destined for great things in your life then it's time to commit and do what it takes to get there. This process is not going to be a bed of roses, but every bit of work you do will be well worth it in the end. When you are able to see clearly and to manifest your dreams you will know why you made a commitment to do the work in the first place.

In the next chapters I am going to lay out the Courageous Process step by step. Throughout all the trials that I have gone through over the years, this has been the process that kept me going. This is also the process that I teach all of the women that I coach and mentor. Your only job is to do the work. Be courageous enough to take the first step and allow the process to guide you.

Now let's Get Courageous!

CHAPTER 5:
STEP ONE – YOUR AWAKENING

Have you ever had an experience, whether small or catastrophic, that alerted you to what was really going on in your life? Maybe you were in debt up to your eyeballs and it hit you dead in the face that something was completely wrong with the way you had been living. This is what I call your awakening. It's the sudden and intense realization that your life is not the way you want it to be.

This may be a hard moment to face. You are probably aware that something is wrong but you don't want to acknowledge how bad it really is. You secretly hope your problems will go away so you can go about your everyday life, but eventually you can't ignore the truth anymore. The problem has gotten so big that it's out of control. Now it's a crisis. It didn't have to get to this point. It's time to stop ignoring the reality of your life, time to stop walking around every day in a daze blind to the vast world around you. Wake up and realize that no matter how bad things may be there is help. There is a way to overcome the troubles you have been facing.

In order to handle your awakening with grace and move forward with your life, you need to acknowledge the reality you are living in, accept responsibility for the condition of your life, practice forgiving yourself and others, and learn how to master your emotions. Let me explain how to do each of these things in detail.

Acknowledge Your Reality

The key to handling the realization that your life may not be all that you want it to be is to acknowledge exactly where you are in life. You have to be real with yourself and acknowledge all the challenges you are currently facing. You might think that by acknowledging your problems you are now defeated, and admitting that things are not perfect somehow means you are no longer in charge of your life. This couldn't be further from the truth. I want to dispel this myth right now. Acknowledging your problems is one of the most powerful steps you will ever take on your journey towards living a courageous life. It will give you the control and the power you need over your life. The simple act of seeing what's in front of you is so freeing. I have seen people go a lifetime without acknowledging the hurt and pain that they feel. On the flip side, I have also seen people who step up with ease to acknowledge that things are not right in their life. These people are able to free themselves from the burden of the pain and get the help they need to live healthy, happy lives. This is what I want for you.

If you don't get anything else from this book you have got to get what I'm telling you now – the act of acknowledging will set you free! You'll be able to move on and begin exploring the life you deserve to have. It will give you the strength to build courage and keep moving day after day even when the going gets tough.

I remember my own encounter with acknowledgment like it was yesterday. It was winter and cold outside. My husband Jamil and I got in our old beat up Chrysler Sebring and headed to our Wednesday night business meeting. I hated that car. Quite frankly I was embarrassed to even be driving it. It was so old and it had a seat pattern that reminded me of a couch that my grandmother would have had in her home in the sixties but it was all we could afford at the time. Another reason I hated that car so much was because it told the truth about where I was financially in my life. Broke.

So there we were heading to our meeting looking all dressed up with smiles on our faces in a beat up car. When we arrived we were greeted by our friendly, empowering business partners and team leaders who we saw on a weekly basis. If you'd had a bad week this was the time to wipe that frown off your face and get the attitude of a winner, and that's exactly what we did. We started to mingle and finally we were all asked to sit down so the empowerment could begin.

I took my seat near Jamil and we listened to the opening remarks, which were the same every week. Then we came to a part of the meeting that I hated. Our leaders would ask all of the team members who had brought a guest with them to stand up and be recognized for their hard work. During this part I always wanted to disappear because for the most part I never had any guests. It's not that I didn't want to bring people to the meeting but I had a hard time getting people interested enough in the business that they would want to come. I must admit sometimes I didn't even try. I wanted to be successful in the company but something just wasn't clicking for me. Something was missing – my passion for the business.

After all the guests had been identified they were escorted into another room so they could hear all about the business op-portunity. For the rest of us, this was when the empowerment zone began. We started off with another part of the meeting that I hated, the time when all the people who had actually been doing the work got recognized and rewarded. Don't get me wrong, I was happy for the people who were successful, but it only made me feel worse about myself. Why couldn't I get it together and make success happen for me?

Soon the recognition portion was over (thank God) and it was time for the leaders to really dig in and motivate us to go out and do better. I loved this portion of the meeting. For as long as I could remember I had wanted to become a professional speaker, and I wanted to be the one up on the stage motivating everyone to go out and do their best. There was something about being in front of a crowd of people telling them how to improve their lives that appealed to me. As I listened to the speaker that night I drifted off into my own world, daydreaming about being one of the top players in the company. I imagined that I was making all the money they promised I that I could make and taking lavish trips, and that I was the one doing the motivating. It was wonderful. I told myself that as soon as I made it big in the company I would earn the right to be the one up on that stage motivating everyone.

Then I heard a lot of commotion. People were clapping and cheering with excitement! I had been daydreaming for so long that I missed the entire meeting. It was now time for the close. This was when everyone who had invited guests tried to persuade them to join the business. If you were like me and Jamil and you had no guests, this was yet another awkward moment of the night. As all the people who had brought guests took them to the side to hear their decision Jamil and I were politely encouraged to come over and have an impromptu meeting with our leader. This was yet another one of those moments that I hated because I knew what we were going to talk about. He wanted to know why we didn't have any guests. After I gave my same old lame excuse of not being able to persuade anyone to come he began to give us our own mini empowerment session about how we could do it and how much money there was to be made. I loved the idea of making all the money they promised, I just didn't want to do the work it took to make it.

Finally all was said and done, and Jamil and I got into our beat up car and headed home. Something was wrong, terribly wrong, not with Jamil but with me. Something about that evening just didn't sit right with me. I began to ask myself questions: Why am I in this business anyway? If I say I love this business why am I not making money in it? Why am I not willing to do what it takes to be successful at this business? As my car was pulling into my driveway something happened. It was like something had hit me right on the head. I realized that my life sucked. My reality was that I hated the business I was in, and all I really wanted to do was speak. I wasn't making any money in the business which was causing so much financial strain on our household it was unreal. Our home was in foreclosure, our cars had already been repossessed, we were dead broke and I was totally unhappy! It was at that very moment I had the courage to confront and acknowledge the truth about my life. That night was pivotal, because that was when I decided to quit the business and start my own speaking company, Kiki Ramsey International. That night I decided to pursue my passion.

Acknowledging that my life sucked was one of the hardest things I ever had to do. Nobody wants to say that their life sucks. But I knew that if I were ever going to reach my goals in life it was high time to be honest with myself. Now it's your turn. It's time for you to face the reality that your life may not be exactly what you want it to be. Its ok; the only important thing now is that you fully acknowledge the truth so that you can move forward with your life.

Accept Responsibility

I must admit that accepting responsibility can be a hard thing to do, but it's an imperative part of the courageous process. It doesn't matter if the hurt and pain in your life was caused by you or by someone else. Accepting responsibility carries no blame. Just because you accept responsibility for something doesn't mean it's ok that this thing has happened to you; it only means that you are acknowledging that it happened and it's your burden to carry no matter what it is.

Let me tell you why accepting responsibility is so important and why it actually works. When you accept responsibility for something that has happened to you, it means you are taking back the hold that thing or situation has over you. When you choose to place blame on someone or something for what happened to you, the situation has control over you. You are essentially saying that because you are not willing to accept responsibility for your life you are going to allow another person or the situation to control your actions and your responses.

You've seen this happen before. People who play the blame game are always playing the victim role. These people can never get ahead because they blame other people and things for the state of their lives. How in the world is a person supposed to get out of the victim cycle if they continue to blame others for their downfall? The truth is as long as you blame other people or situations for the things they have done to you, you will forever be held captive in an unfulfilled life. The only way to truly release yourself from captivity is to accept responsibility that something happened to you and you have to do what it takes to overcome the situation. When you fully accept responsibility you are saying, "I acknowledge that this thing has happened in my life. My life may not be what I want it to be at this moment, but this is my story to carry and I am willing to do what it takes to overcome this no matter what." You may have to go through this process more than once, but the sooner you start acknowledging the wrongs and accepting responsibility for them the more powerful you will become.

That night when I was pulling up to my house after the empowerment meeting I had to accept that my life was in its state of affairs because of my own doing. I was broke, facing foreclosure on my home and unhappy because I chose not to do the work in my business or change my situation. I couldn't blame my business leaders or my partners for this. At that moment I had to sit in my mess and accept that it was my burden to bear. But that was not the first time I was faced with accepting responsibility.

For many years I blamed my mother for all the things that were wrong with my life. Because she was a drug addict, it messed up my childhood. It was her fault we didn't have enough money to live in a big house like my other friends. If she had been a better mother, I wouldn't have gotten pregnant at sixteen years old. I blamed her for my bad attitude because I thought that if she weren't so screwed up I would have been a happy child instead of an angry one.

One day during my freshman year of college I was talking with a close friend. I had been whining and moaning about how bad my life was and how much I hated my mother. I was telling him all my sob stories about how she ruined my life and how much I felt I was at a disadvantage because I didn't have a better mother. I talked about how much my mother's drug addiction affected my life and how I wish she had never picked up drugs. My friend was so patient and calm and then out of the blue he said something I had never heard before – "You need to stop blaming your mother for all these things that have gone wrong in your life. Everyone makes mistakes and you need to learn to forgive her and move on. Besides, you only get one mother." At first I was shocked and hurt by those words. I'm telling him how hurt I am and all he can say is that you only get one mother? Then I took a minute to ruminate on what he said. He was right. I realized for the first time that my mother was only human and she was not perfect. I wanted to put my mother up on a pedestal because there is this idea of what a mother should be, but not all mothers are created equal. My mother was who she was and I was going to have to accept that fact if I ever wanted to move forward in my life. I had never looked at my situation that way before. Somehow it didn't seem right to place so much blame on her anymore.

The process was long and hard but I began accepting responsibility for my life. Yes, my mother was still a drug addict, and yes, my childhood was less than perfect, and no, it wasn't me that caused all these things to happen in my life – but I had to accept that this was my life and my story. God wasn't going to magically give me another mother and make everything right. This was it and I could either sink or swim, continue to deny or choose to accept. Luckily for me I chose acceptance and I continued the process of healing.

Practice Forgiveness

Every time I say the word forgiveness people give me this deep look of sadness and frustration. I'm pretty sure that's because forgiveness is a word that carries so much weight. Why is this word so heavy and what does it have to do with the awakening process? The reason we are talking about forgiveness now is because acknowledging your hurts and accepting responsibility for the state of your life will most likely bring up a lot of feelings that you have been trying to avoid.

To tell you the truth, most people either don't want to forgive or don't know how. I have encountered many women who have not come to the point in their lives where they want to forgive the person who has caused them so much pain. It's just something they cannot wrap their minds around. On the other hand I have coached women who have come to me because they desperately want to know how to forgive but don't know where or how to start. I've even coached women who desperately need to forgive themselves but that's an even harder concept to grasp.

Forgiveness is a process of letting go and surrendering all the blame, hurt and pain you have experienced in life. When you choose not to forgive, you allow your pain to control your life and you become powerless. But when you decide to forgive it actually releases the pain that has been holding you hostage for all this time. I'm not saying that after you choose to forgive you will never feel pain in the future, but by forgiving you are not allowing the pain, the situation or the person to control your life. You are saying, "I have the power to move on with my life and this thing will no longer dictate how I feel and what I do in response to my situations." Forgiveness is such a powerful thing!

It is important for you to think about forgiveness as a journey and not something you do in one day to get it over with. It will take some time and that's ok. As you travel along this road you might find that there are several people that you must forgive. These people could include your family members, colleagues and friends, but the person who is most important in this process and yet often the most unnoticed is you. That's right, you need to forgive yourself.

Day after day I see women beating themselves up for something that happened in their past or that is still happening in their present. Does this sound like you? Chances are it does. Because I have experienced this and I am a woman I know that you are probably harder on yourself than anyone else. It's time to stop the self-abuse. If someone else were treating you this badly, you would be angry. You are only human and you are allowed to make mistakes. It's ok that things don't always go right. Forgiving yourself is absolutely necessary for you to move on. You are the most important asset in your life, and if you are beating yourself up all the time how do you ever expect to accomplish your goals? When you realize you are not perfect and you give yourself room to make mistakes you give yourself a shot at a great courageous life. Once you forgive yourself you can move on to forgive others.

I know all too well that sometimes you don't want to forgive others who have wronged you, and I'll admit it can be a very hard thing to do. However, forgiving them is what begins the healing process and allows you to start releasing all the pain, hate, and ill feelings you have towards the person. Remember forgiveness is a process and it will take you some time to get through it.

I could not have made it through the years with my mother's substance abuse problem and all of the pain and the hell she put me through without forgiveness. The only way we maintained the close relationship we had was because I chose to forgive her for all the less than perfect experiences I had to endure. It didn't excuse her for all the pain she caused but it did set me free. It allowed me to see her drug abuse for what it truly was – an addiction. When I forgave my mother it helped me to focus on helping her through her addiction instead of wallowing in my own pain – a far better use of my time and energy. It also gave her more reasons to fight to free herself from her addiction, because she knew that no matter what, her daughter was going to be by her side. You want to know something funny? The help I began to give my mother all those years ago made me who I am today, and this is why I'm able to help thousands of women through their pain, including you.

The importance of forgiveness was also evident to me when I decided to quit my first business. You might be wondering, "Well, who did you have to forgive in that story?" I had to forgive myself. All the time I was in that business I was beating myself up on a daily basis because I didn't have the motivation or drive to do the work necessary to succeed. Every week I would go to the meeting and leave feeling more depressed than before I had got there because I knew I hadn't done the work. But when I had my moment of realization and decided to quit, I had to forgive myself. I was giving myself permission to grieve the loss of my perceived success in that company and to move on and explore my true passions. I no longer wanted to beat myself up for not doing work I didn't want to do in the first place. It was such a freeing experience and it allowed me to move forward with my goal of starting a new company.

You might be saying, "Ok, I understand forgiveness and why I need to do it, but how do I forgive? Where do I even start?" To help you with this process I have a powerful exercise for you to do once you get to the Courageous Action section of this chapter. I have had countless women do this exercise and their breakthroughs have been amazing!

Master Your Emotions

One of my favorite sayings is, "If you learn to master your emotions you learn to master your life." Too often as women we lead with our emotions. I'm not saying that having emotions is a bad thing. (If that were the case I would be in big trouble.) However, when we allow our emotions to guide our actions we are yet again giving over the control of our lives. When it comes to your emotions it is your job to accept responsibility for how you respond to certain situations regardless of how you may feel about them.

When it comes to mastering your emotions you must know that we all experience positive and negative feelings. No one is immune, but how you respond to your negative emotions will determine how successful you will be at overcoming the obstacles and challenges you face in life. Here are some examples of negative emotions that you have probably experienced:

Abandonment, fear, anger, defeat, disappointment, hopelessness, frustration, loneliness

This is just to name a few. There are hundreds more that I didn't write, but you get the picture. Each one of these negative emotions has the tendency to hold you back from your dreams and aspirations. That's why it's so important to learn how to overcome negative emotions so you stay on the road to courageous living.

As I mentioned I have experienced each of the above emotions and I had to figure out a way to push through them during hard times. Through research as well as trial and error I have developed a process that will allow any woman, including you, to master your emotions. These steps are simple yet powerful, and together they make up the final step in the awakening process. Once you have completed this step you will be so proud of yourself and you can move on to step two in the Courageous Process.

How to Master Your Emotions:

1. **Acknowledge Your Feelings**

   You will see the word "acknowledge" throughout this book because it's very important. It is imperative that when it comes to mastering your emotions you don't try to ignore that you are having negative emotions about a situation. Ignoring the feeling only intensifies it. Acknowledge that the feeling is there so you can deal with it.

   Let's say you get angry because your spouse spills coffee all over the floor and decides not to clean it up. You come home to find this huge mess on your carpet and you are left to deal with it. This scenario would make anyone angry, especially if you have light colored carpet and you appreciate a clean house. This is a time that you should acknowledge that you are angry. When your spouse arrives at home don't pretend you're not mad because it will only make matters worse in the future.

2. **Identify the Underlying Message**

   Sometimes your emotions are telling you something deeper than what's seen on the surface. Ask yourself, "What message is this emotion trying to send me about my situation?" Your emotion could be trying to tell you that you are truly hurting from a prior incident.

   In our example you are going to have to assess if you are mad at your husband because he left the coffee spill on the floor or if there are some underlying issues, negative feelings, or problems that have not been addressed. If there are issues that you have not dealt with this is the time for you to recognize them and deal with them in that moment. Gather all your thoughts and sit down to have a very open and candid conversation with your spouse.

3. **Don't Allow the Feeling To Control You**

    Just because you are experiencing a negative emotion doesn't mean that you have to give it full control over you. Remember that when you allow something to control your life you are literally giving away your power to make your own decisions. When you experience something negative you have the option to decide that you are the one in control. This gives you the power to handle any situation in a productive manner.

    When you are confronting your spouse about the coffee spill on the floor you will remain calm and cool because you are in control of your response. In other words your response is your responsibility. You are responsible for the way you handle any situation you may encounter. This would be a great time to practice talking with a monotone voice, and there should be no yelling. If you handle this situation in this way you should get a lot further with finding a solution to the issue.

4. **Begin Positive Self-Talk**

    Positive self-talk helps you fight against all the negative programming that you have learned over the years, and it gives you a new outlook on life and how to overcome your emotions. When you change what you say to yourself from negative to positive your negative emotions begin to heal. At the very moment you are feeling a negative emotion you need to begin speaking words to yourself that empower you to address the situation in a more positive way. Tell yourself you can handle what's in front of you and reaffirm that with more positive self-talk.

There you have it, the four simple steps for controlling your emotions. If you practice these steps you will become a master of dealing with difficult situations.

Now you have a great tool box on your side for handling your awakening and taking steps to improve your life, rather than burying your head in the sand and ignoring your problems. Taking the actions in this chapter can be a difficult and emotional process, but it will help you so much in getting back power over your own life. You are now prepared to move forward with your courageous process.

Courageous Action Step:

A. Forgiveness Exercise

You are going to write letters to the people you need to forgive in your life. I personally think you should first write a letter forgiving yourself and then write to someone else if you need to. The person you write this letter to can be alive or dead, because sometimes we hold on to pain and blame even after people are gone.

Start the letter off with Dear _____. Write the actual name of the person in the blank. Then proceed writing this letter by getting anything you want to off your chest. Tell them why you are upset or hurt, and explain to them how what they did affected your life or how it changed you. This letter is for you to get it all out. I want you to know that there is freedom in releasing this pain from yourself.

At the end of the letter I want you to write this sentence – "And I forgive you." Wow, what powerful words! You have a choice and you can decide to let it all go and forgive.

Once you have written the letter and gotten it all out don't be afraid to release whatever emotions come along with writing this letter. You may experience tears, anger or severe pain. Don't suppress your emotions. This is a purging and freeing experience and it's ok to express your feelings.

When you are finished with your emotional expressions feel free to tuck the letter away in a safe place. I suggest you reread and repeat this process of emotional expression because as I mentioned the process of forgiving is not automatic. If you don't want to hold on to the letter because it brings up bad memories, let me offer another suggestion. When you have finished writing your letter, tear it into little pieces, and with every tear say, "And I choose to forgive you."

Repeat this exercise for every person you need to forgive. After you do this exercise it's time to celebrate because you have just released yourself from a heavy weight. I want you to remember that forgiveness is a continual process. Just because you forgive doesn't mean you forget, it simply means you are choosing not to hold on to what has been done to you and instead you choose to move forward.

B. Answer these questions in your journal:

1. What and when was your moment of awakening? How did you handle it?

2. What is your reality right now? Have you fully acknowledged and accepted your reality?

3. Are you ready to accept responsibility for your life and all that has happened in your life?

4. What negative emotions get the best of you at times? Are you ready to master your emotions?

Courageous Lessons Learned:

It's time to wake up! The moment you realize that your life is not what you want it to be is called your awakening. During your awakening you must acknowledge your reality, accept responsibility for what's happened in your life, practice forgiveness and master your emotions. Doing these things builds up your courage muscle and prepares you for the steps to come.

CHAPTER 6:
STEP TWO – MAKE A DECISION

Are you aware that your life is one decision after another? From the time you were a toddler and started forming your own thoughts you began making decisions. The choices you made when you were younger might not have always been the right ones, but you learned over time what was acceptable and what wasn't. By now I'm sure you are aware that your ability to make decisions about your life and your life's direction is one of the most important things you can do to move yourself ahead.

In my years of coaching, I've seen many women have a hard time making decisions as it pertains to the direction of their lives. If you are unable to make important decisions, you simply float through life drifting in and out of situations that are presented to you, never being in control of your own destiny. You allow others and the societal norms to make decisions for you.

When you decide to be fully present in your life you will want to make all the decisions about how you live. You will want to be in complete control of the direction in which your life goes because the decisions you make determine how you will live your life.

What Do You Want?

When you are making a major decision about your life, you need to answer one of the most important questions you will ever ask yourself – "What do I want from my life?" Wow! This is a very simple question, but it holds so much power. I have found that many women do not know what they want from their own lives. Whenever I ask a room full of women how many of them know exactly what they want, less than half of them raise their hands. Why is that? It's because we as women have been so conditioned to take care of others' needs that we put ourselves on the back burner. We are simply too busy a lot of the time to think about what we want out of life. The busyness that we experience is certainly understandable; with taking care of the children, the spouse and the career, who wouldn't be busy? But it's time to stop and ask yourself the important questions. Do you want to continue to live your life on auto pilot, putting everything and everyone before yourself? Or do you want to experience a big amazing life that up until now you have dared only to imagine? If you chose the latter then it's time for you to answer the biggest question: What do you want? What do you want for your personal life, your career and your family life?

This question may be hard to answer. As women we tend to look at what other people are doing to measure what we want for our own lives. Sometimes we gravitate towards other women and what they have done because they have made it to a certain success level that we want to achieve. We say to ourselves, "They are super successful and I want to be just like them, so I should do what they are doing." Then we go about trying to emulate their actions. But here's the truth about doing that – you are not being authentically you. When you base your life on what someone else has decided to do with her own life there is no room for creativity and no room for you to be who you were meant to be. These successful people have taken time to discover themselves and their own unique gifts, and what you are attracted to is their results. You can have similar or even better results if you take the time to understand what you truly want for yourself. We don't need another imitator. The world is dying for originality, and it wants you and all your uniqueness and splendor.

I know if you are anything like me you admire some of the most successful people because there is no one else like them in this world. These people are highly successful because of that very fact. So here's what you need to do: spend some quiet time with yourself. Find a place with no TV, no books, no radio, and no distractions so you can think about your life and what you really want out of it. I want your thoughts to be uninterrupted and uninfluenced by other things. Sit back and get very quiet and still. Think about the life you have right now and think about the life you want to have. Ask yourself a few questions.

- If money were not a factor, what would my life look like right now?
- If money were not a factor, what career would I pursue?
- What do I truly want out of life?
- What are some things that I have been dying to do?
- Where do I see myself in one year? In five years? Ten years? Twenty?
- I have always wanted to _____.
- My dream is_____.

By answering these questions, you have just discovered what you want out of your life. That is major! Now you can move forward with a clear idea of what you want your life to look like.

The Importance of Direction

When you understand what you want from life, you can map the direction you want to go. In order to get to what you want you have to know where you're going. The problem I have seen is most people start out on a journey with no destination, and if you do this you will end up nowhere. That's where you'll find half the world, in the land of nowhere, just roaming around with no real purpose or destination. This is not where you want to be. When you find yourself with no direction bad things are bound to happen. For example, have you ever seen a teenager who had so much potential get caught up doing bad things? This is because they had no real direction or destination for their life. Have you ever wondered despite all the bad things that have happened in their lives why some people continue to thrive and make positive progress? It's because despite all those bad things they had direction and a destination they were headed towards and they were determined to get there.

This reminds me of how I made it to college despite living in a house with a mother addicted to crack and a baby on my hip. I was so determined to make it that I refused to allow my circumstances to hinder me. I had a destination I was trying to get to and I had a one track mind that led me straight to college where I learned, developed and grew into an amazing woman that I eventually came to love.

I ended up in college because I made a decision. That night when I was sitting on the couch in the crack house, hating my mother and her addiction but most of all hating what my life had become, I vowed that my life was going to get better. I made the decision that no matter what bad things happened, I was going to be successful. As I said before, this decision has been with me my entire life. It is why I made it to college, why I made it to grad school and got my PhD, why I started my two businesses and why I continue to empower women all over the world. I started with one little decision.

I have a saying that goes, "Everyone can make a decision to go up or down, left or right. The decision is yours. Which will you choose?" I had the option a long time ago to choose right or wrong, up or down, and I thank God I chose to go in the right direction. So can you – it's as simple as making a commitment to yourself to do the right thing and make the best choices.

What Are You Willing to Give?

Once you make a decision about what you want in life, you are not done yet. I wish it were that simple. There is one major component that everyone tends to leave out when it comes to making a decision and that is deciding early on what and how much you are willing to give to get to your goals. This is so important because it prepares you to be strong in the face of adversity. What do I mean by this? As I have already mentioned, you will go through adversity while trying to reach your goals. It's a fact, but most people just don't want to face it. Whether you acknowledge it or not you will face trials and challenges on your road towards success. The clear question is, what will you do when you face them?

This question can be easily answered if you decide what you are willing to give to reach your goals. If you can get it in your mind that you are willing to go through whatever it takes then you are going to be in a good place when challenges inevitably hit. This will help keep you from giving up on yourself and your goals in life.

I was so determined to make it that I didn't care what challenges came my way. I told myself I was willing to go through hell or high water not to be a product of my circumstances. That night when I was sitting on that couch in the crack house I not only made a decision to succeed but I also prefaced that with a promise. I told myself that no matter what bad things happened in my life I was going to be successful. With that statement I prepared myself to keep going through any troubles that showed up in my life. Did bad things continue to happen? Of course they did, but I refused to let them break me and I refused to break a promise to myself. I might have forgotten my promise from time to time, but I always came back to it because it meant something to me.

So I ask you, what are you willing to give? Are you willing to go all in even when things get tough? This is the promise and the decision you need to make today. You need to tell yourself that you are 100% in it to reach your goals and you will never quit or give up no matter what lies ahead. This is going to be the best decision you ever make.

Courageous Action Step:

A. Make Your Decision: Decide right now what you want out of your life.

Answer these questions in your journal:

- If money were not a factor, what would my life look like right now?

- If money were not a factor, what career would I pursue?

- What do I truly want out of life?

- What are some things that I have been dying to do?

- Where do I see myself in one year? In five years? Ten years? Twenty?

- I have always wanted to _____.

- My dream is _____.

B. Revisit your promise to yourself – the one you made in the Courageous Action Step from Chapter 1. Make the decision right now to stick by your promise and stand up to the challenges and fear that you face. Make a decision to unleash the courage that you have inside when a difficult situation arises. Remember that this is the most important promise you will ever make, and if you hold onto it through the storms you will come out on top.

Before we move on to the next step in the Courageous Process I just want to take a moment to congratulate you because most people never make it to the point of decision. This is a big deal and you should be proud that you are making progress on your journey towards being courageous.

Courageous Lessons Learned:

Making a decision about what you want for your life is one of the most vital things you can ever do. The most important question to ask yourself is, "What do I want?" After you have figured out want you want you must then figure out what you are willing to give to get there.

CHAPTER 7:
STEP THREE – DISCOVER WHO YOU REALLY ARE

Finding out who you are is the biggest puzzle you will ever solve. Once you discover the real you, you'll wonder where you've been hiding all these years.

You may not be aware of this but it takes real courage to discover and accept your true self, and to be vulnerable enough to show the world who you really are. The reason this can be so difficult is because most of us don't understand ourselves and hide behind what we think we should be presenting to the world. We tend to take on the persona of what our parents, friends or other family members want us to be. Many of us women hide behind clothes, makeup or a less than authentic attitude trying hard not to show the world who we really are or what we really feel because we are too afraid that they will judge us and not like us. We don't want the world to see us naked and barefaced, or to see that we want to give up on our dreams at times. Instead we present ourselves as having it all together, but deep down we are hiding behind a mask, afraid to show who we really are to the world and to our own selves.

It's time to stop hiding! It's time to discover who you really are. I know from experience that feeling like you don't know who you are or who you were meant to be is a terrible feeling. It's like wandering through the world with no real purpose. Well, I'm here to tell you that your life has purpose and the real you is what the world is waiting for.

Reflecting on Your Story

You can discover a lot about who you are by examining your story. We all have been conditioned by our life stories. You may have had a great childhood and didn't face a lot adversity growing up. This is the story of many women I know. However, you might have had a very rough childhood, such as I did, and faced many adversities growing up. It doesn't really matter which type of childhood you had; in either situation you were raised with a set of circumstances that now play a major part in your story. Your experiences and the choices you have made throughout your life made you who you are whether you are fully aware of it or not. By exploring these facets of your life you will gain a deeper understanding of what makes you, you.

Reflection is one of the best ways to dig into your story. The core meaning of reflection is to think deeply. In my years of coaching and mentoring women I realized that reflecting can be a hard process for some women because it can bring up a lot of unwanted emotions and memories. However, reflection plays a big part in finding out the root cause of why you act the way you do or why your life is what it is. Another reason reflecting can be so hard for women is it forces them to take the time to sit, be alone and think. This sounds simple but many women are so busy helping and taking care of everyone else that they barely ever have time to take care of themselves. For some of us sitting still and being with our own thoughts quite frankly scares us. I understand this dynamic so well because for years I ran from my own thoughts, hiding behind the business of my life. It wasn't until I was desperate to understand who I was that I sat down and took the time to discover the real me. Now it's your turn. It's time to look back over your life and pick out some key memories, circumstances and experiences that may have caused your pain and your happiness.

When I first took the time to reflect over my life, let me tell you it wasn't pretty. I was sitting down one day thinking about my childhood, how I grew up and why I am the way that I am. As you know I was raised in a house with a mother who was addicted to crack cocaine and many nights I slept on a couch in a crack house while my mother was upstairs getting high. None of these experiences are pleasant memories but the fact is they are a part of my story and my reality. I am the daughter of a drug addict and for years I was ashamed of this and hated to admit this fact. It wasn't until I learned to be honest and vulnerable that I was able to release my fears about what others would think and say about me. Throughout this process I had an epiphany. I realized no matter how much I hated the fact that I was the daughter of a drug addict and my childhood sucked, nothing was going to change that. I was always and forever going be the daughter of Alberta Turner and my childhood and all the experiences that shaped it were mine to keep. This is the only life and the only past that I get. I couldn't change it. In that moment I realized that all my experiences were made exactly for me and they are what made me who I am today. Had I not had a mother who was addicted to drugs I might not have become the daughter who desperately tried to help her change her life, which in turn became a passion for me to help other women change their lives. All your life experiences are intertwined and can work for good if you allow them to. Let me tell you right now that your experiences have made you who you are too, and together we are going to explore the good and the ugly. Now let's start your reflection.

Remembering

It's time to dig deep and remember circumstances and experiences that have happened in your life. I'm going to ask you some very specific questions that will open the gates to allow you to remember things about your past both good and bad. All of your memories may not be pleasant but remembering painful experiences is a part of the reflection process. When you remember something unpleasant, don't try to suppress the emotions you feel. As long as the emotion doesn't require emergency attention, try letting the feelings flow as you move through the reflection process. One of the reasons we don't know who we are is because we are too afraid to allow ourselves to feel unwanted emotions. It's ok to feel and once you get out the tears or the anger you may feel better. During this process you are also going to remember some amazing experiences. These experiences along with the negative will shed a lot of light on your life story and who you really are.

If you want, you can consider this entire chapter one big Courageous Action Step. You may find it helpful to journal about your answers to the questions that follow. Or you may simply want to reflect on them in your mind. Do whatever is most beneficial for you. As we go, I'll reflect on my own experiences as an example for you to work with.

What is your very first memory? This question is so important because it puts the framework together about how far your conscious mind goes back. When I ask people to do this some of them can go as far back as three or four years old. There is no wrong or right answer to this question. The memory might not even make sense and it may or may not even mean anything in the long run but it's important to know. What comes to mind when you think about being a child? Do you remember any certain smells, places or experiences? These memories might be a little hazy but just do your best.

My first memory has never made much sense to me. I was about five years old and I was attending my mother's wedding, which was held at my grandmother's house. I remember being all dressed up in a very pretty dress and my hair was curled with a bang in front. I remember loving bangs. My mother had on a baby blue wedding gown and a white veil. I remember crying and hanging on to my mother's leg for dear life because I didn't want her to get married. She was marrying my sister's father; however he was not my father. I have no idea why I didn't want her to get married. I can speculate that I didn't want my mother taken away from me, but I was five so I have no clue. Incidentally they split a couple years later but they never got divorced. I don't know the significance of this memory, but that's ok because it's not important that you know the meaning of every single thing you can remember. However, it might be different for you. You might be able to connect your first memory to something that is significant in your present life. Remember the goal of answering these questions is to help you explore your story and to connect some of your experiences that make you who you are.

What was your overall childhood experience? It is important that you answer this question from your own memory and not what you remember being told. As a reminder during this entire reflection process you must try to get everyone else's thoughts out of your head and begin to think for yourself. It's time to formulate your own thoughts and opinions. With that being said, how do you view your childhood experience? Remember there are no wrong or right answers here, there's only truth and reality. What specific things or events do you remember about your childhood? Were your parents or guardians nice to you? Did your family have money or were you poor? These are just some questions to get you started.

Overall times were pretty hard for me as a child. I remember wishing I was living in a dream because I did not want my reality to be true. As far as I can remember my life was pretty good up until around the time I turned ten years old. Prior to that I can't remember any significant circumstances or situations either bad or good that have shaped me. When I was ten I found out my mother had a drug addiction, and from there everything went downhill. I loved my mother so much and during that time I couldn't understand why she would allow something like drugs to destroy our life. At times she was such a strong woman, but at other times she was so weak that she couldn't help but to succumb to her addiction. There were days that I would literally beg her not to go buy drugs. These were conversations no mother and child should ever have to have, but that was my reality. As time passed I became more angry at her and at the world. I felt like I was in a dark place and I didn't know how to get out.

What were your teen years like? The teen years are some of the most challenging for many people. This is because of the difficult transition that begins to happen between childhood and adulthood. Most people begin figuring out who they really are despite what they have been told when they reach their teen years. Most of the time we also remember these years better than we remember our childhoods. Now is a great time to dig down and really pull out some significant experiences in your life. Did you have it easy or hard as a teen? Did you like school? Were you the popular kid or were you picked on? Were you an introvert or an extrovert? Were you self-motivated or lazy? Did you battle with any emotional problems?

As I said, I became angrier and angrier as I grew older. As a teen the darkness only got worse, and because of my angry disposition I felt like I didn't have to listen to authority, especially my mother. I began rebelling against everything she would tell me and I certainly wouldn't tolerate any discipline she would try to give me. I hung out with friends all night doing all kinds of crazy things. Worst of all I began looking for love in all the wrong places and in all the wrong ways. Deep down I think I knew my mother loved me - she told me that she did all the time - but she was never able to kick her addiction which I considered the true test of love at the time. Therefore I couldn't feel the love I'm sure she wanted me to feel. Truth be told I felt unloved and numb. I hated those feelings. I wanted so much to be loved by my mother, by my absent father, by someone. I wanted so much to have a normal life but those were not the cards I was dealt.

I began to medicate myself with sex. Unfortunately the promise of love sucked me in to one too many beds, and I never found what I was searching for. All of the guys that promised me love turned out to be one disappointment after another, and with every unfulfilled promise a piece of my heart was taken away. Out of all these unfulfilled promises of love, one left something that forever changed my life. At sixteen years old I found out I was pregnant! This news turned my life upside down.

"There is no way in hell I'm having this baby," I told my mother when she made me take a pregnancy test. I didn't want to bring a baby into the hell that I was currently living. It was bad enough to have to fight like hell for myself, and there was no way I wanted a baby to be subjected to such anguish and misery. There was only one way out of that situation for me and that was to get an abortion, but I had no money. I set about with determination to get the $400 that the abortion would cost, and I was able to collect all the money I needed but it took me a while.

As my mother and I pulled up to the abortion clinic I saw protesters picketing, holding up signs and screaming all sorts of things that I couldn't quite make out. When I got out of the car all their slurs became very clear to me. They were saying things like "Don't kill your baby," and "You are going to go to hell." The things they were saying were so obscene, but all I could think about was how terrible it would be to bring a baby into my reality. My mother and I rushed past all the protesters and made our way into the building. We both were visibly shaken by that experience and my mother looked at me and asked me if I was sure I wanted to go through with this. I told her yes without any hesitation. Although my mother still had her drug addiction she was always there for me, and during this moment I needed her and was so glad she was there. I filled out the paperwork, paid the money and waited. Then my name was called. This was it. This was my time to turn the clock back and set at least one thing right.

As I climbed up on the table to be checked I felt a nervousness in the pit of my stomach. I had never done anything like this before but in my mind there was no question that I had to do it. As the doctors began to check me I closed my eyes praying for it all to be over. After everything was complete one of the doctors asked me to close my legs, open my eyes and sit up. There was no way it could be over that fast. It didn't even hurt. The doctor looked at me and said, "Well, you most certainly are pregnant. However, you are too far along for us to do an abortion for you in this clinic." All the life drained out of me and I burst into tears. Through my sobs they were able to tell me that I was about seventeen weeks pregnant and in the state of South Carolina they were only able to do abortions up to about eleven weeks. They told me there were other options for abortions in places such as Georgia, or I could consider adoption. I was still crying uncontrollably as they ushered me out to the waiting room where my mother was now standing looking very alarmed.

She rushed over to me and through my sobs I was able to tell her what had happened. She held me, consoled me and told me everything was going to be ok. We finally gathered our things and headed towards the door. I was not ready to face the mob of people outside but there was no other way around it. Once outside I began to hear the angry screams of the mob – "Baby killer!" I remember thinking about how harsh these people were. Across the parking lot was a family planning clinic. How convenient right? My mother wrapped her arms around me and tried to protect me from all the protesters as she headed straight to the clinic. As we proceeded I heard some of the slurs in the crowd begin to get a little more positive, like they knew I had not gotten the abortion and now they were cheering. However, I tried to pay them no attention because I was still in shock from the whole experience.

In the family planning clinic we met with a nice lady who educated us about all our options, including keeping the baby and adoption. Up until this point I had never had a doctor's appointment for my pregnancy because I had always been adamant that I was getting an abortion. Now I was faced with the possibility that I might have to raise this child in this hell of a life that I was accustomed to, or better yet give my baby away.

After all the craziness of that day I finally got time to think about the situation in its entirety and I still came up with the same answer: there was no way I wanted to bring a baby into my world, so I set out to find $800 to go to Atlanta GA to have an abortion. I also went into a state of denial. In my mind there was no reason to tell people I was pregnant because I was eventually going to have an abortion anyway. I set about doing my normal activities. I joined the cross country team as I did every year. We would run about three to four miles every day and after each run I would go over to the grass and throw up. When the coach would ask what was wrong I would tell him that I ate something that upset my stomach. No one knew I was pregnant because I was not showing at the time. I even went as far as to try out for the basketball team, but for some reason I broke down and told my coach and she immediately put a stop to that. If I'm being truthful with you I was secretly hoping something happened to the baby so I didn't have to go through the drama of having an abortion.

Somehow the rumors began to spread throughout the school that I was pregnant and people began to talk. I grew more and more anxious about having the abortion. I was trying to come up with the $800 but it just wasn't happening. I tried everything I could and called everyone I knew but none of my family or friends had any money they could give me. One day I was sitting at home with my mother arguing, ranting and raving about getting the money for the abortion, and finally she'd had enough of me and my madness. My mother took me by the shoulders and shook me until she got my attention. She said, "Look here girl! You are having this baby whether you want to or not. Obviously God wanted you to have this baby because you have done everything in your power and you still have not been able to get rid of it. You are going to stop acting crazy, you are going to take your butt to the doctor and you are going to have this baby and I am going to be right here with you." As the tears began to roll down my face she took me in her arms and hugged me.

You'll be happy to know that after that I finally accepted the fact that I was going to be a mother. I started going to the doctor and had my first appointment at five months. Four months after that I delivered a beautiful baby boy, Tomazye'. Now that I was a mother I shifted all my focus to protecting my baby from the crazy world I lived in. There was no way I could allow him to grow up like I did, so that meant I had to make some major changes. Fortunately I was able to graduate from high school and go to college to get a higher education. Once I graduated from undergrad I went and got a master's degree in Social Work. I eventually went and got a master's in positive psychology and now I have a PhD in Business Psychology. I count my blessings every single day and I know my experiences as a teenager played a big part in making me who I am today.

What were you told about your future when you were growing up? Were you told that you could do anything and become anybody, or were you told that you were a nobody who would never amount to anything? Some of these things may have stuck with you throughout the years. Try to remember what you were told so that you can put it in perspective as it pertains to your current life.

Contrary to what you might think I was never told anything negative about my future. My mother always told me that I was smart and that I could do anything or be anything I wanted to be, and my teachers told me the same. Ironically a lot of the time I didn't feel like I could live up to this because of my situation growing up. How could I trust what my mother was telling me if she couldn't even get her life together? My circumstances and experiences had caused me to think negatively about my future. In spite of that I chose to latch on to what my teachers and other people I deemed successful had to say. I believe this and my raw inner strength got me through.

What circumstances or experiences have affected your adult life in a major way? Your childhood experiences do make up a major part of your story and who you have become today, but we must not forget about your adult experiences. It's time to start thinking about some of the major experiences you've had since becoming an adult. These experiences have a major place in your story and can explain a lot about your current circumstances.

I consider my adulthood the time from college to the present. Even though sometimes in college I didn't feel like an adult I certainly had to learn to act like one. This is where I truly began to grow into a woman. I learned all kinds of lessons, from how to love unconditionally, to coming to the realization that you can't help everyone (I still struggle with the latter). Making it through college with a baby in tow was the truest test of perseverance of all.

I knew college was somewhere in my future from the moment I made my promise to my ten-year-old self. However, I didn't have good enough grades after high school to get into a four year college, and I had an infant son to take care of. Luckily

I had amazing people by my side such as my Godmother Brenda Guy. She took me to her alma mater, a small college in Kentucky called Berea College, and she showed me that even though I wouldn't be able to realize my dream of going to a Division 1 school to run track and field, I could still get a college education and most importantly I could take my baby with me. This opened my eyes up to a whole new world.

Because I didn't have the grades to get into Berea College right away, I went to community college for a year. I did my very best, got good grades and was accepted into Berea the very next year with a full four year tuition-free scholarship. You can't imagine how excited I was when I received that acceptance letter. When the time came I packed bags for my baby and me, and we moved to Kentucky where I didn't know a soul. I knew my future and the future of my child depended on me getting a proper education.

The next four years would be some of the hardest and most rewarding of my life. I learned to stop being an enabler in my mother's life, even though it was very hard for me to do. Because of my passion to find solutions to help my mother I changed my major from business to family studies. I wanted to learn more about helping people in need. Oh and truthfully I also failed Accounting 2 and that scared me and gave me more ammunition to change majors.

I learned to be a good mother. My college had so many resources and I can honestly say that my son grew up in the best environment possible. Tomazye' loved Berea. Everyone knew him, and he ran around that campus like he owned it. He was even on the track team with me. He would go to every one of my meets and sit in the stands in his Berea track uniform and cheer me on. Being able to raise him in such a positive environment gave me the parental tools that I needed to be the best mother I could be.

I also learned the true meaning of friendship. I met Kisha, one of my dearest friends, while in college. We are still close to this day.

I was finally able to graduate after four long years and I couldn't have been more proud of myself and my accomplishments. On graduation day I walked across that stage with Tomazye' right by my side. He had survived college right along with me and there was no better way to share this experience than walking across the stage with the person I loved most. I was the first in my immediate family to graduate from college. This day was so special and one of my biggest accomplishments.

I left undergrad ready for the next phase of my life: grad school. However, that experience was also with its challenges. I wanted to be a little closer to my home in Greenville SC, so I wanted to go to the University of Georgia in Athens. Berea was a five hour drive from home, so UGA was a good compromise. In order to apply to UGA, I needed to fill out the application, send in my transcripts and take the GRE. The first two were easy, but that wasn't the case when it came to the GRE; standardized tests and I just don't get along. I didn't get the score that I wanted to on the test, but my grades and GPA from Berea were stellar so I didn't think I had a problem. I was wrong. While the specific program I applied to, the School of Social Work, accepted me, I got a denial letter from the college itself.

You know I didn't allow this to stop me. My friend Kisha and I sat down and drafted the best letter in the history of appeals if I do say so myself. I received word that I had been granted a hearing at the college. I got a babysitter for Tomazye,' and I drove to Athens, GA, from Kentucky for my appeal hearing. When it was my turn, I was called into a room where there were about 8 people seated around a large round table. For twenty minutes I answered question after question as to why I should be accepted into UGA, and you better believe I had an answer for every question. After the hearing was over I went to the bathroom before getting back on the road to Kentucky. While I was washing my hands a woman walked in. I recognized her as one of the panel members. She looked at me and silently mouthed something. I squinted my eyes to see what she was saying and she repeated herself very quietly – "You got in." I began to scream and splash water, so she put her finger to her mouth and softly said, "Shuuuush." I quieted down immediately but it was so hard to contain my excitement. "I did it, I actually did it" was all I could think about on my nine hour drive back to Kentucky. This experience taught me that no is not always no, and you have to fight for what you want in life because it is not always going to come easy.

While I was getting set to go to grad school, I had another life-changing experience – a very positive one. On Valentine's Day, I was surfing the internet to see what singles did to celebrate the holiday. I ended up on Match.com and decided to give it a try. I created a profile and looked for matches in the area close to UGA, finally settling on Atlanta because there were more choices. There was one guy that caught my eye, because his profile said "I am a Godly man looking for a Godly woman." That totally attracted me, but after Valentine's Day I had forgotten about Match.com because I was busy getting ready to graduate and head to grad school. It wasn't until I had moved to Athens and was checking my email one day that I remembered, because Match.com had sent me a list of my top ten matches and the same guy was still there on the list. Now I had a dilemma: in order for me to talk to this guy I would have to pay a membership fee, and I had never done anything like that in my life. I contemplated it for several days until I saw an episode of The View and they were setting one of the cameramen up on a date with someone from Match.com. That very day I decided to pay for one month and one month only. If I emailed him and it didn't work out, oh well.

So I emailed him and luckily for me he turned out to be the nicest guy. We emailed for a while until I was comfortable enough giving him my number, and after that we would talk on the phone for hours. Then we met in person and decided to start dating. I had never been treated so well by any man in my life. I was in awe of him. We fell in love and that next Valentine's Day, six months after we met, one year after I first saw his face, he proposed. We were married a year after our first meeting and we have been happy ever since. That is quite a story but it's true. Being married to my husband Jamil has been one of the greatest joys of my life. Sure, we have had our ups and downs, but overall it's been an unforgettable ride and I wouldn't change it for the world.

Now that you have dug deep and gotten a good glimpse into your story, I hope you have started to connect some of the dots between your experiences and who you are. But we are not done yet. In order to complete your self-discovery, you must learn to analyze your story and your experiences.

Analyze Your Story

There may be many things hidden in your story that you don't recognize right away. Analyzing your life can help lead you to discovering the meaning and results behind your experiences. For instance when I began to analyze my story I was able to connect that I became a social worker because I spent all my life trying to figure out how to help my mother get off drugs. I was drawn to the helping professions like psychology and social work because I needed to understand how the human mind works and what makes us do the things we do. I felt like if I could understand human behavior then I would be able to help my mother break free from the hold drugs had on her. These are the kinds of connections I want you to make in your story, because they help to explain who you are.

Here are some questions to guide you through this process of analyzing your story. Feel free to journal your answers or to contemplate them internally depending on what works best for you.

1. **What childhood circumstances or situations affect your life today?** This question is key because as you have explored in the previous remembrance exercises, there are probably several things that happened in your childhood that still affect your life today. You may not have realized it before because you were never asked to examine your life in this way. These circumstances and situations could be the very reason you act the way you do right now.

    Wow, I don't even know where to start when it comes to analyzing my own childhood! There are so many connections that I have made from my childhood experiences that have played a major role in me being who I am today. I think the most important one is the fact that my mother was addicted to cocaine. I honestly think that had my mother not used drugs my life would be totally different. Through this experience I developed both positive and negative traits. One of my negative traits is I have a very angry side. Over the years I have learned to control my anger but as I was growing up I was a holy terror. My closest family members could probably tell you some stories. I'm also a control freak. This has been one of the hardest things for me to rectify as an adult. I learned to be controlling because as a child a lot of responsibility fell on my head. I was making decisions at twelve that many grownups never have to make even for themselves.

    But on the flip side of things my childhood also taught me to be super caring. I want to see everyone prosper. In particular I don't like to see women suffering and that's because I hated to see my mother suffer. Besides her addiction, she had to deal with undiagnosed depression and anxiety, trauma and even domestic abuse. It hurts my heart to remember all the pain she had to endure. I know for a fact that the reason I chose to go into the helping field and become a social worker and ultimately a positive psychologist and executive coach is because of this experience in my life.

2. **What problems are you experiencing today that were also present in your past?** Many of your problems are not new. They are the same problems that have been recycled throughout your life. They keep arising time and time again because instead of actually solving the problem you sweep it under the rug. It's time to explore those issues.

My anger has followed me all my life. As a child growing up in my situation I learned to be very angry, so angry that I would scream, yell, curse, throw things, and even fight. I can remember getting into several fights throughout my middle, high school and college years because I didn't know how to control my anger. My anger even caused problems in my romantic relationships. I knew I was going to have to get my anger under control if I wanted to live a decent life and have good relationships with my family and friends, so I put in a lot of work to become a master of my emotions. I'm not saying that I'm perfect and that I don't get mad on occasion, but nowadays I try to handle my anger in a more productive way. My goal is to continue working on this issue until the day I die. I'm sure you also have an issue that you will have to keep working on throughout your life. Don't beat yourself up about it. Just resolve to become better with each test. I'm a living witness that it does get better.

3. **Do you have a positive, optimistic outlook on life or a generally negative, pessimistic outlook? How does this current attitude relate to the attitude you had growing up? How does this attitude relate to your life right now?** Your attitude about life plays a huge role in who you are and how you interact with the world and the people in it.

Analyze your current and past outlook on life and see what connections you can make.

I have always been a mixed bag of emotions, but I'm sure I would not be where I am today had I not had an optimistic outlook on life. I have been through a lot and I have had to learn that despite my challenges I must stay positive. My optimism has allowed me to be persistent and keep pushing towards my dreams. On the other hand, despite popular belief I can be very pessimistic at times. Just because I'm a positive psychologist and executive coach doesn't mean I don't feel down once in a while. I'm only human and when times get really tough I tend to get down just like any person would. The difference between me and other people is when I notice that I'm being negative or pessimistic I try to turn that around as soon as I realize I'm doing it. It's easy to get down about your situation when things go wrong but you must become a person who is in control of her emotions and turn it around for yourself. One of the techniques that helps me is thinking about all that I have to be thankful for. Despite all that I've gone through I have so many blessings to count, and I bet if you picked out the things you are grateful for you would say the same thing about yourself. Your attitude is what you make it. Yes, you may have developed a negative attitude from your past, but your future attitude is your choice. Every day I wake up and choose to be positive and have an optimistic outlook on life, and you can too.

4. **What do you believe about money and what were you taught as a child?** Money can be one of the biggest issues we struggle with as adults. What you learn about money when you are young can shape how you handle your financial future and ultimately your life. Analyze what you were taught about money when you were younger and see if you can make any comparisons to how you handle money as an adult.

I had major problems with money in my adulthood. I never seemed to have enough, and if I got any I would spend it immediately. For the life of me I couldn't understand why I did this, but then I analyzed my story. My family was pretty poor growing up and my mother was on welfare so you would think that every bit of our money was spent to buy the necessities, but that was far from the truth. Even though I was taught that money did not grow on trees and was very hard to come by, my mother didn't always do the right things with her money and we always seemed to run out before the end of the month. I hated those times because we were always scraping to get by. However, my mother always provided us with awesome gifts for Christmas, birthdays and special occasions whether she could actually afford it or not. My sister and I would get things like Nintendo's and stereos, but we only got to play with them for a little while because after few weeks my mom would pawn them. She always promised to buy them back but most of the time we never saw them again. My mom would also give me money on occasion and because I was a saver I would never spend my money. When she found out she started borrowing the money back from me and I never saw it again. That's when I stopped saving and began spending everything she gave me right away so she wouldn't come take it back from me. I carried this spending habit into my adult life, and it took me a long time to realize my money was safe now and no one was going to come and take it. That might seem silly to you, but my spending habit was a subconscious reaction. I knew intellectually that no one was going to take my money but it had been embedded in my mind that I needed to spend it before it was taken away, and I was still reacting to this years later. You may discover something similar in your past. Chances are you have been reacting based on something that has happened in your past. It's time to put together the pieces of your life and figure out why.

5. **What do you believe about health and fitness and what were you taught growing up?** Health and fitness is another major area that follows us from childhood, which we may or may not realize. Were you active as a child? What types of things did your family eat? All of these things may play a part in why you are in your current health state.

For as long as I can remember I have been on the go and full of energy. My mom used to say I came out of the womb running. To this day my friends and family say that I don't know how to sit still and they are right. I always loved sports, too, and my favorite is running. As I mentioned, I ran track and field at school and won all kinds of medals. I even became the second in the state for the 800 meter run during my junior year in high school, which was one of the highlights of my life. Despite the fear that I couldn't do it because I was a single mother and full time student, I also ran track and field all four years of college. I still love to run and participate in 5k's, 10k's and half marathons! I also love going to the gym. There is something about getting a great workout in that makes me feel so good about myself and my day.

Now eating healthy is another story, although I have come a long way over the years. You have got to understand that I am a true southern belle which means I grew up on soul food. My mother really knew how to cook and she taught me all of the secrets of the trade, both good and bad. I grew up eating a lot of fried and greasy foods and subsequently this is the way I learned to cook. The worst part about not eating as healthy as I should is that I have never been one to gain a lot of weight. I have teetered between the same ten pounds here and there as long as I can remember, so I don't get the same consequences as other people do and this makes it harder for me to comply. Even though it is hard I know my family depends on me so I not only have to cook well for myself because it's the right thing to do, I must cook well for my family too. I have changed a lot of my cooking habits. I no longer cook vegetables out of a can; I only use fresh or frozen. I have cut down drastically on the fried foods and substituted baked foods instead. I cut down on all the oils and margarines that I use. Although some of the changes that I've made to my diet have been difficult it has certainly been worth it.

6. **What do you believe about going after your dreams?** Were you taught to dream big and that the sky is the limit or were you taught to think small and be realistic? Were you taught to find a good job and keep it forever or were you taught to be an entrepreneur and create the work you want to do?

As I have said before no one blatantly tried to discourage me, and my circumstances alone were enough to give me the determination and motivation I needed to push towards my dreams. Everyone saw something in me, something in my eyes. I never understood what people meant when they said, "She is so determined, she is going to get her way no matter what," until I grew older and realized that I was the kind of person that would let nothing stand in my way. I think because I faced so many hard challenges in my life I had no choice. If I was going to get the life I dreamed of and that I saw others living, I was going to have to be so determined that I let nothing stand in my way. If you are able to find this type of determination you will certainly be able to manifest anything you want in your life.

7. **What were your religious beliefs? Did you grow up having a spiritual practice or believe in a deity or deities?** Did your family ever go to a place of worship? Or were you never introduced to religion? How has that changed or affected your life today?

There has always been some type of reference to God in my life, ever since I was little. My mother didn't take us to church all the time but we did go on occasion. She would talk about God and I knew through her that there was a higher power. My fondest church memories are of the times when the bus would come around my neighborhood when I was younger to pick us up and take us to church or revival. It was so fun. I got to hang out with my friends and even meet new ones. We always got awesome snacks and juice, cookies and chips. This made me really love going to church.

I believe that I had a great introduction to religion early on in my life. Over the years I got wiser and began to grow and build a relationship with God. I began to see Him as the person who could supply all my needs. Even though I went through so much drama, eventually I knew that He was there for me despite any hard situation I might face. It took me some time to get to this place in my life but I'm so happy I got here and that I can depend on Jesus for everything.

8. **Do you have great romantic and non-romantic relationships in your life?** Are you married or do you want to get married? If you are married do you get along with your partner or are you divorced? Were your parents married or divorced? Or did you live in a single parent household? Do you attract certain people in your life, good or bad? If so, why? Do you have a great relationship with your parents/ guardians and your children? Could it be based on what you experienced as a child? Was your father present or was he absent in your life? Did your father treat you like a princess or was he mean and cruel? Was your mother absent or present in your life? Did she treat you amazing or cruel? How have these various situations affected your current life? Do you see a pattern between what you experienced growing up and what you experience now?

My relationships have been one of the most defining things in my life. The way I learned to relate to my mother dictated how I behaved as a child and how I behave now. I learned both good and bad ways to relate based on my relationships with my mother and non-existent father. I had an epiphany through analyzing my story and therapy that my mother taught me love was based on words and not actions. Over time I realized that my mother truly did love me. She told me she loved me a lot but as I was growing up her actions, namely using drugs, said something completely different. I needed to believe she loved me; therefore I chose to believe her words and not her actions. This type of belief has haunted me for many years. As a teenager I chose to believe that when a guy said he loved me he really meant it despite his actions of cheating and lying. This led me on a path to destruction and I ended up being hurt by more men than I care to explain. This type of thinking was very destructive and harmful. Things didn't change for me until I met a man who believed that love was an action and not just words. Lucky for me that man became my husband.

The fact that my real father never claimed me played a big part in the way I looked for and found love. My stepfather was in and out of my life growing up but his love was very distant and difficult to understand. Therefore prior to my husband I never felt like I had a man truly mean it when he said he loved me. Needless to say it has been a long and hard transition but by the grace of God I learned to have healthy relationships in my adult life in spite of my trials.

9. **Did you have a lot of drama in your household growing up?** Were things unstable and chaotic? Or were things calm and peaceful? How does this differ from your life right now? Did you keep the same ways or strive for the opposite?

I guess you can imagine that my life was pretty dramatic! Between my mother and her addiction, taking care of my younger sister and my baby and my stepfather's craziness things were chaotic. I learned to function so well in an atmosphere filled with drama that I began to crave it in my adult life. I once asked my husband prior to getting married why we didn't argue. He looked at me and asked me if I wanted to argue. Part of me wanted to say yes because that is what I had always been used to but I told him no because I knew that was the answer I was supposed to give. Arguing and drama had become a way of life. If there was no drama I felt like something was wrong. I thrived off of it. As you are reading these words you might know exactly what I'm talking about if you are anything like me. I have had to learn healthy ways of communication. It has been difficult but my real goal has always been to live in harmony with my spouse and children and that meant I had to do some work on myself and my behavior. If this type of drama reminds you of your life, it means you have some work to do too because living in chaos is not the way to go.

10. **Was your family emotionally attached or emotionally removed?** Did your mother or father love and hug you or was there not much physical affection going on? How does this differ and relate to the way you are currently? Are you emotionally available?

I am a very emotional person, and I want to be loved. Physical touch is the main way I received love when I was younger; therefore that is the way I give love. Despite all her shortcomings my mother was a very affectionate person. She would always hug me, kiss me and tell me that she loved me. I ate this attention up and it made me feel so good. I believe this is why I am such an affectionate person today. I will kiss and hug on my children and husband because this is how I like to display my love and it's what I was taught.

11. **What things were you told about life that you have been holding on to until today?** You might have grown up in a very negative household where you were told that you

would never amount to anything, and now you continue to tell yourself that you will never amount to anything and you are not worthy of having a great life. What has been holding you back?

For many years I secretly told myself that I was not good enough to find the love of my life, or to have an amazing life, because of my past. During my dark days I would sabotage any opportunity because of my negative beliefs. In these moments I had to recognize what I was doing and correct myself. It took me course-correcting a thousand times and doing a lot of soul work before I got it right. I now know that I am worthy and I am more than enough. Allow me to be the first to tell you that you, too, are worthy and you are more than enough. Whatever has been holding you back, it's time to let it go and walk into your purpose in life. Your destiny is waiting on you to catch up. I want you to declare that the very thing that has been holding you back will hold you back no more.

12. **What is your overall attitude about life right now and why is it like this? How were your parent's attitudes about life in general?** Right now you have developed a general attitude about life. What is it? By now you should be able to pinpoint some specific things that have occurred in your life that may have caused you to think like this.

Overall I have a very positive outlook on life. I know that I have the power to manifest anything and everything I want out of this life if I keep moving forward and putting in the necessary work. Over the years I have gained several different philosophies that I live by. One of my main philosophies is that there is always a way. I believe no matter what you want to do or become there is always a way if you are willing to do the work and find it. This has really served me well over the years and I lend it to you to adopt for yourself. You will be amazed at how true this is when you open yourself up to all the possibilities.

13. **What are your true values? What things do you care about the most? What things did you care about the most growing up?** When we grow up we learn to value or not value certain things in life. Think about those things and see how they fit into your life now.

Even though I grew up in a difficult situation with my mother it never stopped me from wanting to be around her or my family. Now I know we all have some sort of crazy family story but the truth is none of us can choose our biological families, so I have learned to value my family. I love being around them even when they are acting crazy. I also value my spiritual connection with God. When you are younger it's hard to understand the vastness of God, but as you grow into adulthood it gets somewhat easier to understand that God is almighty and able to answer all of your prayers. As an adult I have been able to do so many things that I never imagined because God has always been on my side. It is amazing to see how far I have come.

14. **How does your life differ now than when you grew up?** You are now an adult! So is your life completely different now than when you were growing up? What are some areas that have improved or changed? What has not improved or has stayed the same?

My life is totally different than when I grew up. I made my promise to succeed and that's exactly what I have done. I saw the effects that drugs had on my mother and I knew I would never use drugs. My goal was to live a good and successful life. In my immediate family we do not have all the drama I grew up with and I am thankful for that. For the most part my life as an adult has been pretty good compared to where I come from.

15. **If you could change anything about your life what would it be and why?** You can be honest with yourself here. This is not a judgmental question. This question is here to guide

you into figuring out some of the choices and/or situations in your life that you would like to see changed. At times many of us wish we could have made different decisions during a period in our lives.

If I had asked myself this question before I started doing all my work I would have about two or three pages including all the things I have mentioned in the above paragraphs. But now that I have done my work I don't wish to change anything about my life. On occasion I wish I were smarter and that I'd never had to encounter some of the things in my past, but that kind of thinking gets you nowhere. I hope you see by answering all these questions and analyzing your story that the things that have happened in your life were meant to be. You must ask yourself this question: If you were to truly change something about your past what would your life look like today? Sure you have things to work on and things could be better but your past can help you grow if you allow it to. From now on let's focus on your future and let the past propel you forward.

Wow, you did it! You have analyzed your story! All these questions have helped you see deeper into who you really are and why you do some of the things you do. If you completed this exercise to the fullest, your head is probably reeling from all that you have discovered about yourself. These new insights can be huge so don't take them lightly. Take a minute to absorb all that you have discovered. Let it sink in. You have just broken through some major barriers and roadblocks in your life, and this is such an amazing accomplishment. Through this exercise you have discovered the essence of who you really are. Now it's time to summarize it all.

Courageous Action Step:

Answer this question: **Who am I?**

Based on all the questions you have answered about yourself, write out a statement that explains who you currently are. You can take excerpts from the questions you have already answered. This statement can be as long or short as you would like. There is absolutely no wrong answer here.

Here is my example "Who am I?" statement:

Who is Kiki Ramsey?

I am passionate, loving, caring and authentic. Although I have been through a lot of hurt and pain, I am very optimistic about life. I am super determined to succeed at what I put my mind to. I am super complicated and I am perfectly human. I am a mother, wife and daughter of God. I am worthy. I am Kiki Ramsey.

Courageous Lessons Learned:

Knowing who you are is the biggest puzzle you will ever solve in your life. Once you discover the real you, you'll wonder where she has been hiding for all these years. To gain the full picture of who you are you must analyze your past experiences and dive into the choices you have made based on those experiences, because your life story is what makes you who you are today.

CHAPTER 8:
STEP 4 – IDENTIFY THE REAL PROBLEM

You have come so far and I really want to commend you for doing the work. The process of changing your life is not easy, but it is so worth it. I want to remind you to keep up the good work as you continue to press past your fears and towards your purpose.

The next step of the Courageous Process is identifying the real problem(s) in your life. This is a difficult step because problems can come from anywhere and anything. What manifests itself as a problem in your life may not be a problem for the next person. That doesn't make it any better or worse, wrong or right, for you – but it's up to you to solve your problems, whatever they may be.

Surface Problems vs. Root (Real) Problems

Your real problems may be covered up by all the pain, hurt and lies you have experienced in your past. You might think you know the problem but the real question to ask yourself is, what is the underlying issue that has caused the problem? Typically we see the way the problem manifests on the surface, but we don't take the time to deal with the root of the problem.

Surface problems manifest in the emotions we feel when we're experiencing something difficult. This includes outward shows as well as internalization of emotions. The root problem is based on past experiences. It is the trigger that causes our display of surface problems. It is important that you learn the difference between the two so you can identify what to focus on when trying to solve your problems.

Here are some examples of surface problems (SP) vs. root problems (RP):

- A person may be defensive and mean (SP) as a byproduct of being bullied as a child and never learning how to channel anger (RP)
- Low self-esteem (SP) as a byproduct of emotional abuse (RP)
- Anxiety (SP) as a byproduct of growing up in a chaotic home situation (RP)

Over the years I have had many surface problems that I have tried to deal with without ever knowing the root problems. One of my major issues when I was younger was promiscuity. If I'm being honest with you I slept with several guys because they told me they loved me, which was all I wanted to hear. I thought that if they told me they loved me it must be true. At that time in my life no one had to prove to me that love was more than just words.

This became a cycle for me. I would meet a guy and get close enough for him to tell me he loved me and then we would have sex. After sex something between us always seemed to go wrong or change. Either he would cheat on me or just stop talking to me all together. I couldn't figure out what was going on. I didn't understand how anyone could lie about something as important as love. I learned that not everyone took their words as seriously as I did. It took me a long time to get the picture, but I eventually figured it out and wised up. I realized that love was much deeper than words and that deepness is what I was missing and longing for in my life. In my case my surface problem was promiscuity and my choice to sleep with different guys to get what I thought was love. The root problem was that I was missing love and a deeper connection from my mother and father, and therefore I was trying to fill a void in that area of my life. Any time you are trying to fill a void, you most likely have a real problem in that area.

Do you see how this works? Getting to the root problem is one of the most important parts of your journey towards courage and finding your purpose in life. We all have difficult challenges to face in our lives, but sometimes we never solve the issues because we don't know the real problem. When you are able to identify your real problems and deal with them accordingly you will be able to make a shift for the better in the way you think and how you live your life.

Identifying the real problem can lead you to face some deep emotions and situations that you may have otherwise ignored. It takes real courage to bring up some of these issues and deal with them. The stuff that we bury deep in our souls has been buried for a reason, and when you choose to face those things you must draw upon all your strength to get you through. It's a necessary evil that will turn out in your favor.

Are you ready to identify your root problem? It's time to sit down and do some more work. Let me help you by breaking common problem areas down for you so you can take a look and see what kinds of surface problems are manifesting from the root issues in your own life.

Six Common Problem Areas

I have been helping women with their problems for over fifteen years and throughout all my research and studies I have noticed that women have the most trouble in six areas of their lives: emotions, health and fitness, spirituality, relationships, finances, and career. I bet if you look at your life you will see that many of your problems have stemmed from one or more of these areas. In order to have a well-rounded life it is important that you figure out where you stand in each area. It is equally important that you figure out in which area your biggest challenges lie.

Emotional Wellness: People who are emotionally well are able to cope with their feelings, thoughts and behaviors, both positive and negative. Your ability to manage your emotions has a lot to do with your overall feelings about life. For example if you allow a particular thing to always get you upset then this could affect your overall happiness in life. To be emotionally well you must manage your feelings in a healthy way on a consistent basis.

Good emotional wellness includes:

- Managing your feelings during difficult situations
- Practicing healthy ways of relaxation
- Communicating your feelings appropriately
- Thinking positively
- Adjusting to change
- Adjusting to failure
- Building self-confidence and self-esteem
- Putting your needs first

Physical Wellness (Health and Fitness): Physical wellness consists of being physically fit through regular exercise and eating a proper diet. Being physically well can lead to great benefits such as more energy, a longer lifespan, greater self-esteem and more overall happiness about life.

Good physical wellness includes:

- Maintaining exercise on a regular basis
- Getting routine health check-ups and screenings
- Eating a balanced diet
- Avoiding drugs, tobacco and alcohol
- Getting enough sleep
- Maintaining a healthy weight
- Practicing good hygiene

Spiritual Wellness involves the search for meaning, purpose and significance. It is your ability to establish peace and harmony and your ability to integrate your beliefs and values into your actions.

Spiritual wellness includes:

- Meditation or prayer
- Compassion, the capacity to love and forgive
- Gaining fulfillment through your beliefs and/or faith
- Defining your faith, values, beliefs, principles, and morals
- Finding meaning in life events
- Connecting to a deeper part of yourself
- Developing a purpose in life
- Caring about others and being willing to serve

Relationship Wellness: All human beings strive for love, support and human connection. Positive relationships with our family, work partners, friends and community are a very important part of our everyday wellness. Good relationships can improve all aspects of your life, strengthening your health, mind, soul, and need for connection with others.

Relationship wellness includes:

- Staying involved with others by talking about the important things
- Getting through conflict safely
- Communicating appropriately
- Relating to others
- Building trust
- Practicing compassion and empathy
- Forgiving

Financial Wellness: Financial wellness is having an understanding of your financial situation and goals, and being prepared to grow and to deal with any financial challenges that may arise.

Financial wellness includes:

- Understanding the state of your finances
- Saving
- Making wise decisions about money
- Planning for retirement
- Using credit wisely
- Budgeting properly

Career Wellness: The career that you decide on plays one of the biggest and most important parts of your life. Being able to choose a satisfying career has everything to do with your overall life satisfaction.

Career wellness includes:

- Choosing a career that makes you happy
- Choosing a career that challenges you
- Adjusting to new environments and situations
- Making a satisfactory wage
- Making a contribution to the world in which you live

These six categories may be vast but as I have said before there is a good chance that the problems you will identify in your life come from one of these categories. When I look back on some of the biggest problems I have faced, nine times out of ten they come from one of these common problem areas. Knowing these categories is not enough; you must learn how to identify the real problems in your life by differentiating your surface problems from your root problems. Let's give it a try.

Courageous Action Step:

Surface Problem   Root Problem

Think about your current life and all the problems you are facing right now. Find a place in your journal with plenty of space and label two columns, one with the words "Surface Problem" and the second with "Root Problem", as shown above. Then write all the issues that you are having right now in your life in the column labeled "Surface Problem". Don't take a lot of time to think about it because I don't want you to confuse yourself trying to separate surface from root problems at this point. Most of the time we are more aware of our surface problems anyway. Then in the second column labeled "Root Problem" write out the root cause of each problem you listed in the surface problem column. This is going to be a real eye-opening experience. Some root problems may be easier to identify than others.

You might need to really think about this. If you need help, try going back to step three in this process where you had to analyze your story.

Now I would like for you to look at all the problems you have identified and place them in one of these six categories.

- Emotional

- Physical (Health and Fitness)

- Spiritual

- Relationships

- Financial

- Career

Once you categorize your problems, count the number of problems you have in each category. The category that you have the most problems in is the area you need to pay the most attention to in your life. This is the area that has caused you a lot of pain and if you can focus your energies on fixing the issues in that area you will begin to experience a healthier, happier life.

Courageous Lessons Learned:

Surface problems are those issues that manifest themselves based on a root problem that goes deeper to the heart of the issue. The key to identifying the real problems in your life is identifying that true root issue in your life and dealing with it accordingly.

CHAPTER 9:
STEP 5 – DEVELOP A NEW AWARENESS

In the last step you learned what your real problem(s) have been all along. Was it shocking to you? Have you known but didn't want to admit it? Does it hurt? That exercise was meant to help you understand the source of your problem. Although these realizations may hurt, they are necessary for you to get to your goal of discovering your purpose and living a purpose-filled life. You might be thinking that because you know what your true problems are it's time to take some action so you can move on with your life, right? Not quite yet. In this next step of the Courageous Process you have to come to a new awareness about your life and your future.

So what do I mean when I say "come to a new awareness"? To really move forward with discovering your true purpose and following your dreams, you have to develop new ways to be aware about your life and what you can accomplish. Awareness is fundamental to all human activity. It is the basis of your mental state, including creativity, perception, knowledge and culture. It is the portal between consciousness and the world around us. Being aware of what's wrong in your life means that you are conscious of a problem versus continuing to ignore it. On the flip side, being aware of what's right in your life allows you to use that knowledge to encourage yourself and push forward to the next level.

Let's look at it this way – at the very basic level you are aware that you do certain things like making coffee, driving or reading. While you engage in these activities you are aware that you're doing them, but you probably don't pay them much attention. It's as if you're doing them on autopilot. This is considered a low level of awareness. However, when you do a high-engagement activity, such as learning to ride a bike or drive a car, your awareness level is high. You have to be fully aware in these situations because if not something bad could happen such as an accident. Once an activity becomes more familiar you become less conscious of it. For example, have you ever been driving and realized you are somewhere you never intended to end up? What were you thinking? If you had been as focused as you were when you first learned to drive, that wouldn't have happened. You need a high level of focus and awareness when it comes to opening up to the possibilities of your life.

Let's go back to my earlier story about how I got pregnant at sixteen years old. That whole period of my life was very difficult. Imagine thinking you are going to be able to go to college on a track scholarship, and this scholarship was your only hope of paying for a full education so that you could get out of the hell hole you had been living in your whole life. Now imagine that dream disappearing right before your eyes. This is what happened to me. It didn't matter how well I could run or how smart I was; in my world all the girls I knew who got pregnant in high school never went to college. They worked minimum wage jobs and some of them even dropped out of school. This was a future I never imagined for myself, and even though I was facing one of the hardest moments of my life I still wanted better.

As you know, I tried to get an abortion but it was unsuccessful. I know now it was God's way of telling me that was not his plan for my life, but at the time I couldn't see that. I was hurting, scared and disappointed. I was so certain that I had ruined my life, that I was a failure and would end up like many of my other friends who were working low-paying jobs just to take care of their babies. This is where the miraculous happened. The day my mother took me by the shoulders and said, "Look here girl! You are having this baby whether you want to or not" – that day changed my life. As my mother encouraged me to prepare for parenthood and promised to support me as much as she could, she reminded me that I was strong and that I could make it through anything. I remembered the promise I made to myself so many years ago to be successful. This moment gave me a new awareness about my future and what I was capable of. I knew even at sixteen years old that I was going to have to change the way I thought about myself if I was ever going to fulfill my dream of success. You have to do the same.

You cannot move forward in your life if you continue to allow your past to hold you down. You must embrace a new understanding, a new awareness, about what your life can be. The key to awareness is your willingness to show up in your own life. You have to want to be an active participant: to know what's going on, why things are happening and how to overcome your problems. Gone are the days where you can just sit around watching your life go by, living on autopilot and forgetting that you have the power to make the necessary changes and decisions to create the life you want. When you begin to believe and realize you can do anything you put your mind to, the possibilities become endless.

In order to develop and embrace a new awareness there are certain principles and realizations you must learn and then apply to your life on an daily basis. These are based in building up your belief, especially in yourself, and embodying positivity. If you will commit to keeping these at the forefront of your mind they will help on this road of discovery.

Build Your Belief

It's unfortunately difficult for people to adapt the concept that anything is possible. As an executive coach I work with women all the time to help them discover their purpose in life and this concept is always the hardest for them to accept. Being able to master the concept of "anything is possible" begins with belief, and almost all women who are struggling to find and fulfill their purpose have issues with truly believing in themselves. In order to move forward in life you really have to understand this. It is important for me to instill in you throughout this book that anything is possible, and I mean anything! Believing in this one little statement can take you further than most people will ever make it in life. Believe it or not one of the main reasons so many people don't achieve their best life possible is simply because they don't believe in themselves. They don't believe in the possibility that their dreams could really come true, and what happens when a person doesn't believe? You guessed it, absolutely nothing. If you have a dream that you want to accomplish but don't believe you can, you will never find the courage or the strength to make it happen. If you do believe, then anything is possible!

When I made the decision to move ahead in my life even though I was young, about to have a baby and had a mother who was addicted to drugs, I knew it was going to be hard. The odds were stacked against me. My family had very little money, so I knew the only way I could go to college would be to get a scholarship, and I didn't think that would be possible because I had a baby. Nevertheless, I kept up my faith that God would make a way. At my church my pastor said God wanted me to prosper and I chose to believe him.

As I mentioned earlier it turned out my Godmother Brenda Guy graduated from Berea College, a little college situated in a small town in Kentucky. I had never heard of Berea College and at the time I didn't even know where Kentucky was on the map. She told me that Berea was a place where I could take my son with me and get a quality education. I was a little skeptical at first. I mean, what kind of state has "blue grass" for God's sakes? But I decided to see for myself. My Godmother was and still is a big advocate for the college and every year along with the Urban League she took a group of minority students from the Appalachian region to see the campus during what they call "Carter G. Woodson Weekend". It's the college's effort to serve and recruit a diverse population of students. When our bus pulled up onto that campus I was absolutely awestruck by the huge trees and beautiful brick buildings. That was one of the best weekends I had ever had, and it solidified my destiny. I knew I was going to Berea College.

But there was one problem – I didn't have the grades to get in. Although Berea was very accommodating, it also had a rigorous college entry process. They took the best of the best students and applicants' GPAs had to be up to par. My difficult home life and the fact that I had a baby in the tenth grade made my GPA less then desirable. I was disappointed but I knew what I had to do. I needed to go to community college for at least one year to get my grades up with hopes of applying to Berea and getting in.

As academic achievement became my new mission, my belief in myself kicked in. There were still a lot of challenges in my life: I was living with my mother and her addiction, taking care of my child, and helping my mother take care of my younger sister all while going to community college to make great grades so I could have a chance to get into my dream college. Piece of cake, right? Trust me, I was terrified of what I was up against, but I was even more scared about what my life would be if I didn't have a chance at a great college like Berea. So I went about juggling the impossible. I made the decision to believe that anything was possible.

Let me tell you, just because you decide to believe in yourself and go for it doesn't mean challenges won't pop up in the process. There were several things that threatened my chances of completing community college. One of the craziest things to happen was that I almost got kicked out of for fighting. Yes, fighting. I told you I had a very bad temper back then. But it's a long story and I won't go into details; that's for another book. The important thing is I didn't get kicked out and I am so grateful for that. Through that entire experience I learned that difficult situations will happen and you will be tested to see how badly you want to achieve your goal. This is where your belief and determination separate you from those who don't make it. Throughout community college I remained certain that I was going to make it into Berea. When the year was over I had managed to get a good GPA which allowed me to apply to Berea with a good chance of getting in.

One day I went to my mailbox. Inside was a letter from Berea College. It had been several months since I had applied and I was dying to hear something back. I was so nervous I couldn't even wait until I got back in the house to open the letter, so I opened it right at the mailbox. My hands were shaking so badly as I ripped the envelope open. I peered down at the paper and saw the first word: "Congratulations." I didn't even take the time to finish reading the entire letter. I started screaming and jumping up and down. My heart was pounding so fast. I kept repeating "I did it, I did it!" I was just so thrilled with myself. I know the people passing by thought I must have been crazy but I didn't care. I had gotten into my dream college! Once I could calm down I read the rest of the letter, which not only told me that I was accepted but also that the school had awarded me a full tuition scholarship for all four years. You can't even imagine what seeing that meant to me; not only was I going to college, I didn't have to worry about how I was going to pay. This was one of the best days of my life and it happened to me because I believed in myself and was aware of what my future could be if I tried. For this to happen to a girl who had a baby in the tenth grade, with a mother who was addicted to drugs – I knew from that point on anything was possible.

Do you believe anything is possible in your life? Well it is, but if you are still having trouble with this and don't know how to start believing in yourself here are three concepts that will help you.

Know Your Power

So many women don't believe in themselves because they really don't understand their own power. Power is a mighty force inside all of us waiting to be used to our advantage. Power is your ability to control or influence yourself or others. When you understand that you are all-powerful you'll know that you can control and direct your own actions to get and have anything you want in life. It's actually funny to witness a woman discover her power, because as she begins to walk in her confidence, others really take notice and she gets results.

The key to unlocking your power is your mindset. Your power is controlled from within by what you think. If you think bad thoughts then bad things are eventually going to happen. Earlier in step two I taught you a four-step process to master your emotions: 1) acknowledge your feelings; 2) identify the underlying message your feelings are trying to tell you; 3) don't allow the feelings to control you; 4) use positive self-talk. Understanding the impact of your words is imperative, too. If you can remember to embrace and use these four steps then unlocking your power and believing in yourself will be much easier.

Be Open to Hearing the Truth

When you are trying to build up your belief, you have to be open to hearing the truth about your life. This can also be called receiving feedback. What do I mean by this? What you hear penetrates your mind and causes you to make either good or bad decisions. These decisions can be based off of lies you hear from others or lies you tell yourself. You need to separate the truth from the lies.

You must be open to hearing the truth even if it hurts. Hearing a negative truth about yourself is painful, but even a positive truth can cause pain. This is because when you don't believe in yourself it's sometimes hard to take a compliment or see the good in yourself, even when it's right there in your face. Many times the truth is obvious, but you keep devaluing yourself and ignoring that little voice inside that is trying to scream out from the bottom of the pits that you are worthy. That voice is trying to tell you that you are capable of doing all the things you want in life but you ignore it because you are too scared to accept that it might be true. Sometimes you ask yourself questions like, "If it is the truth what will I do with that? How will I handle this truth?"

This happened to me a lot when I was deep in my process of overcoming my fears and finding my purpose. I didn't want to hear the truth because I felt like once I knew it I was going to be responsible for living up to it. I was no longer going to be allowed to make excuses for myself. And I was right. I had to make a choice, though – either I was going to stand in my truth that I was amazing and awesomely made or I was going to continue to shrink behind a life of mediocrity never fulfilling my full purpose. I just came to a point in my life that I no longer wanted to shrink, and in order to make things different I needed to be willing to hear the good and bad truths about my life. Then I needed to take that information and do something positive about it because I am not my circumstances; therefore I can do anything I want and I can reach any goal. When you are willing to hear the truth and accept your part in it, your belief in yourself will continue to grow.

Be Open to Seeing

The last part of building your belief is you must be open to seeing. All this means is that you have to be able to picture yourself in the very situation that you want to be in. I call this visualizing your dreams. Now I know you have dreams and some of your dreams are big and some small. Either way you need to be able to picture yourself living that dream out to the fullest. When you are able to visualize yourself living your dreams it makes you excited and ready to do what you need to do to make them a reality.

When my dream to be a speaker was still only a dream, there were days when I stood in front of my couch imagining that the room was full of people and that I was empowering everyone in the room with my words. I would go through all the motions. On different occasions I would imagine I was in a stadium filled with people and that I was in the middle of the stage addressing everyone. It was and still is such an emotional and inspiring visualization for me. Some of my speaking visualizations have come true and some have not, and this is why I still do it to this day.

I not only live what I teach to women, I also teach the same things to my sons and daughter. This includes Tomazye, Walter, Mackenzie and Tomazye' best friend Nick whom he considers a brother and have been friends since they were in elementary school. I kind of adopted Nick as my own, although Nick's mom Tammy and I have also become very good friends. I always try to motivate Tomazye' and Nick to follow their dreams who are now adults and have kids of their own. For Mackenzie and Walter, it's a little different of a conversation since they are much younger, but the sentiment is the same. Once I took Nick on what I call a "Vision Stretching Mission." This is when you do something or go somewhere that allows you to experience your vision first hand, thus encouraging you to do what it takes to make it a reality.

On this particular day I had to take Nick to an appointment, and on the way I got an idea. At the time Nick wanted to be an architect and I thought it would be good for him to see the architecture of some beautiful buildings. I took him to see some million-dollar homes that I love. On the way there I asked Nick if he had ever been on a Vision Stretching Mission, and of course he looked at me like I was crazy and said no. Then I told him he was in for a treat.

We walked into the model home and I introduced Nick and myself to the sales agent. She was really nice and gave us all the stats on the homes, telling us to have a look around. As we walked into the first room I could see the stunned amazement on Nick's face. While we walked through the house I pointed out all the little details and he acknowledged how nice everything was. When we entered the primary bathroom both of our mouths dropped open. It was absolutely stunning! It had all white tile and double separate vanities on each side of the room and a grand oval-shaped white soaking tub sitting in the middle. We both dubbed that room our dream bathroom. By the time we made it to the fourth level deck Nick had to sit down on the patio furniture and take it all in. It was amazing to see him respond this way and I knew that at that very moment his vision of what he could do and what his life could be was stretching.

On the way to the appointment we talked all about the house and what he would need to do to be able to afford one like it. His mother Tammy called in on the phone while we were in the car and he told her all about the mission and the house. She was surprised to hear what we had done but confirmed that if he worked hard in school he would be able to afford that kind of house one day. It was a great day and it proved that being open to seeing and visualizing your goals helps you believe in yourself.

Embody Positivity

If you are going to embrace a new awareness about your life, you must embody positivity. This means that you need to try and look at the world through positive eyes much of the time. Sometimes this is easier said than done, and the truth is most people see the glass half empty and don't know how to be positive. My question to you is how do you expect to build this new awareness about what your life could be if you continue to be a Negative Nelly? You can't be prosperous if you continue to exude negativity. You have to throw the negativity away and replace it with something better – optimism.

Optimism vs. Pessimism

Optimistic people look on the bright side of things. They see the positive aspect in all things and they can visualize a better outcome. Optimistic people understand that negativity is all around them but they choose to disregard it and take the positive route. Optimistic people also understand that being positive is a choice that they can make every day. They take responsibility for their positivity.

Pessimistic people on the other hand are very negative and they don't believe that things can get better. They complain a lot and they make excuses as to why things won't work out. They don't even try to hope for the best because they don't want to be disappointed by the outcome if it's negative. Pessimistic people don't understand that they have a choice to be positive. They never take responsibility and they say things such as, "That's just the way it is." Pessimistic people have a way of bringing others down with them. The saying "misery love company" is very true in this case.

Now that you know the difference, which one are you? Are you optimistic or pessimistic when it comes to your future? I can tell you from experience that in order to develop a new awareness about your life you have to become optimistic about fulfilling your purpose.

Why Be Positive?

The first reason to learn to be positive is that positivity offsets the negativity and problems that will occur in your life. When new problems are met with positivity, it creates an opportunity for amazing solutions and breakthroughs to happen. While helping women through difficult situations throughout the years, I have realized that your attitude matters when you encounter a difficult situation. The way you look at the situation and choose to respond makes all the difference in the world. If you see the situation as the worst thing that has ever happened to you then chances are it is going to be much more difficult to get over it. However, if you choose to see the good and want to learn lessons from the situation then it will be much easier to overcome. Having a positive attitude during difficult situations will not only be helpful, but it can change your perspective for good. A new perspective can create an overall positive ripple effect throughout your life.

The second reason to be positive is it creates an overall healthier, stress-free lifestyle. You might not be aware of this but negativity can create stress and stress can cause you to have many health problems, including heart disease or high blood pressure. Negativity also makes it more difficult to maintain good mental health.

The third reason to learn to be positive is you will have better relationships with people. Believe it or not, being a positive person makes people gravitate towards you. If you can be positive people will begin to see that as an asset, and you'll begin to build more good and uplifting relationships, which in turn can lead to many other positive things happening in your life.

Positive Self- Talk Strategies

Being positive has a lot to do with what you say to yourself. When you develop a new awareness about your life you also have to develop a whole new way to talk to yourself. We talk to ourselves all the time, and it is our job to learn the correct way of talking.

Most of our negative talk to ourselves has been taught to us by our past programming. This means we tie our thoughts back to negative things that have happened in our lives, and this comes out in our internal speeches. Most negative programming was taught to you when you were younger, and because you experienced negative images and situations over and over again it made it hard to override. This is why so many people talk very negatively to themselves – negativity has been instilled in their brains. Here are some examples of negative self-talk:

- I just can't remember names.
- It's going to be another one of those days.
- I just can't get it right.
- I just know it won't work.
- I wish this day was over.
- My life sucks.
- Nothing ever goes right for me.
- That's just my luck.
- I'm so clumsy.
- I'm so stupid.
- I'm so forgetful.

These are just a few. If you have ever said any of these to yourself you might not have even realized they were negative. Negative self-talk can be subtle, but strong enough to cause damage. When you talk negatively to yourself you become the result of what you say to yourself. The human brain will do anything you tell it to do if you tell it often enough.

Positive self-talk is a way to override your past negative programming by erasing or replacing it with a conscious and positive new direction. Positive self-talk gives us each a way to change what we would like to change about our lives and look towards a brighter future.

Putting Positive Self-Talk to Work

If you want to change your life, it's time you put positive self-talk to work. Some people call them affirmations. Let's say you want to earn more money. Your earning potential is determined by the limits you set with your own beliefs. If you want to earn more you have to start seeing yourself as worthy, deserving, capable and willing by redirecting your actions and what you say to yourself.

Most people try to figure out how to earn more money before believing they can do it, which is why so many people fail. But another way to earn more money is to believe that you can, and the way to do that is to build up your self-esteem through positive self-talk. Here are some examples of statements you can say to yourself when you want to build your positive self-talk in the area of money.

Example:

- I am no stranger to money. I make money easily.
- Money is not bad. I use money to help people out.
- I never have negative feelings about money.
- I make all the money I need.
- Money is a resource.
- I am a money making machine.

These are just a few statements about money that you can say to yourself. These statements take you out of a negative frame of mind when thinking about money and put you in a positive relationship with finances.

You can build positive self-talk strategies around anything you would like to change about your life. For instance if you want to build your self-esteem, lose weight or just need plain old motivation you can start by using positive self-talk statements.

In order for positive self-talk to work, all your statements should be thought of or spoken in the present tense. This is because you can't focus on what has happened in the past or what you plan to do in the future. What you have control over is what's happening right now. By stating them in the present you are giving yourself more control over your own life and your situation right now. You also have to use positive self-talk on a consistent basis in order for it to become instilled in your brain. Remember that your negative programming has been built up for years and you will never override it if you only talk positively to yourself every now and then. You have to make positive self-talk a habit that never dies.

I hope that you now understand how developing a new awareness will allow you to move forward and create the life that you want. The Courageous Actions in this chapter will help propel you further into nurturing your belief and positivity.

Courageous Action Step:

A. The following questions will help you think outside the box to visualize your dreams and future. Answer these questions in your journal, and feel free to continue to brainstorm and write if you think of additional dream material.

- If you were wealthy and you had all the resources you needed to live your life, how would you start your day? For example, would you start your day with no alarm clock or wake up on a beach? Would you wake up with your children, have time to cook them breakfast, get them off to school and spend the rest of your day doing the things you love?

- What would your entire day look like? For example, would you go into the office and do a job that didn't even feel like work because you were completely passionate about what you were doing? Would you then go home and have dinner with your family and be able to have awesome conversations that don't focus around the lack of money and being able to pay bills?

B. Go on your own "Vision Stretching Mission." This will help you to see or feel your dreams in the flesh. Try going to an open house at your dream home. If your dream home is not for sale, go to one that is very similar. A lot of new developments and luxury townhomes normally have a model home that is open to perspective buyers. You can also test-drive your dream car. This is always fun to do just as long as you can walk away in the end. If you are planning to go back to school take a trip to the college you would like to apply to. Get a feel for the campus. If you want to start a new career see if you can test-drive the career by trying to volunteer for a day. This is a great way to see that career up close and personal. If you are dreaming of writing, speaking, making art or playing music, go see a live show or take in the work of an artist who inspires you. Tailor your Vision Stretching Mission to your personal aspirations.

C. Start a gratitude journal. Take some time each day to write down all the positive things that happened that day and all the things you were grateful for. If something bad happened, try to write down any positive aspects that you found in that experience, such as a lesson that it taught you. This journal will keep you grounded and show you that good things can happen in your life.

D. Write down four positive self-talk statements that you are going to use every day over the next month. It will take a month for these statements to become ingrained in your system.

Example: I am beautiful and I am worthy. Every day I wake up is a new day to show the world what I am made of.

Courageous Lessons Learned:

To really move forward with discovering your true purpose and following your dreams you have to develop a new awareness about your life and what you can accomplish. You do this by building your belief in yourself and embodying positivity throughout your life, which will help lead you into the mindset that anything is possible!

CHAPTER 10:
STEP 6 – CREATE A PLAN

If you dug deep enough and did the work in Step 4 you should have a greater understanding of what's been holding you back from reaching your dreams and goals all this time. With your new awareness from Step 5, you can now acknowledge that you are a smart cookie and you have what it takes to solve your problems. Now that you truly know the real problem you can focus all your positive energy towards finding a solution.

There are many directions you can go when trying to solve a problem. However, I believe the easiest and most effective way to problem-solve is to create a good plan and follow it. In Step 4 you discovered the difference between the surface problems and the underlying root problems that have caused your issues to emerge. In this step you are going to come up with a plan to solve your real problems, which can be a very exciting experience especially if you have been stuck for a long time unable to overcome your challenges. Before we move forward I want to tell you that if you have come this far, you have made it further than most do. Many people get stuck way before they ever reach this step, simply because the work to get here is not easy. But you made it – and now is not the time to give up.

Now let's talk about making a good plan. All plans are not created equal. The strength of a plan depends on how much work, time and research you are willing to put into it. I have made some great plans throughout my life, and I have also made some plans that didn't work out so well. The difference in each plan was me. When I fully committed to the plans they turned out well; when I didn't, things always took a turn for the worse. Making a good plan doesn't mean that everything is going to go exactly as you want it to, so you will need to have some flexibility and adjust if things go wrong. But a plan does give you a good foundation to work from.

In order to make a plan that really works, you have to start by setting some goals. Goals are very important when it comes to overcoming the problems that you identified in Step 4. Goals also play a very important role in helping you reach your dreams and purpose in life. I guarantee that the successful people you admire got to where they are today because they set goals and were able to stick to them. They were able to look at what they wanted out of life, create some goals directly related to that want and stick to the plan. This same process can help you overcome all your problems and live your dreams.

When you begin thinking about your life and the future you want, there are certain questions you should ask yourself in order to start thinking more specifically about the what, how, why and when of your goals:

- What are my real problems? What did I discover in Step 4?

- What do I want to change about my life and my situation?

- What are my career goals? What do I ultimately want to do and become in my career?

- What goals do I have for my family? Where would I like to see my family in one to five years?

- What are some of my short and long term goals?

- What are my financial goals? What are my plans for saving, budgeting and retirement?

- What are my spiritual goals? How do I plan to enhance my relationship with God and/or with the world I am a part of?

- What are my physical or heath goals? How do I plan to maintain or obtain a healthy weight? How do I plan to eat better?

I thought going into this process that I had the answers to all these questions, but boy was I wrong. Before going through and creating the Courageous Process for myself I was very unaware of some of my own shortcomings. When I got down to it and really began to explore the right questions I realized I had so much to learn. For example, I really had to be honest when thinking about my financial goals and my plans for saving, budgeting and retirement. When the question about finances came up I had to think very hard about it. I didn't just want to give any answer so I could move on; I really wanted to give an answer that could help me overcome some of the crazy problems I had been facing and reach my goals for the future. I knew that I wanted to be wealthy but I needed a way to make this goal clearer and easier to reach. Throughout my research I discovered a method that helped me formulate all my goals and ultimately create a great plan for my future. I also incorporate this method when helping a client make goals because it helps us develop a real, viable plan. Now I am going to teach it to you.

The SMART Method

This method is called the SMART Method, created by George T. Doran and I just love the name because it helps us infuse a sense of confidence as you are developing your goals. This is a succinct way to make goals, and it's easy to remember because it uses the letters in SMART as an acronym. Using this method makes your goals more clear and reachable. Let me break it down for you and explain how it works.

S is for Specific

Specific goals have a greater chance of being completed. This means each goal you make should be as specific as possible. The best way to make your goals specific is to answer the questions of who, what, when, where and why.

M is for Measurable

Your goal is measurable if there is a way you can track your progress towards reaching the goal. Ask yourself questions like, "How will I know when my goal is complete? Are there different steps towards achieving my goal that I can mark off as I go?"

A is for Attainable

When you think about a potential goal you first have to ask yourself, is it attainable for you? Is the goal realistic for you? This doesn't mean you should make the goal easy, but it should not be so over-the-top ridiculous that it is unreachable, either. You must be willing to put in the work that is necessary to reach the goal. You must feel that the goal is going to push you to reach higher levels but that it is still within your reach if you work at it.

R is for Relevant

Each goal you set should have your future mission, vision and passions in mind. You want to ask yourself why this goal is important to you. Why do you want to complete this goal? What would it mean to you if you completed this goal? What is your overall mission and vision for your life? Where do you see yourself in one, five, or ten years? Asking these questions gives your goals significance. When you know why you are doing something and it means something to you, you are more likely to complete the goal.

Tis for Timely

Your goals should be tied to a time frame. This gives you a sense of urgency when trying to complete your goal. For example most people would say, "I will lose five pounds." But using a smart timely method it is better to say, "I will lose five pounds in two weeks." This gives you a sense of when this goal needs to be completed so you are not leaving it to chance.

Now I want to teach you how to take your problem and apply the SMART method to solve it. This is called creating a plan. When you are able to create goals to solve your problems you are essentially creating a plan for your life and future. Most people think that this process is difficult, but it is actually very simple. The hard part is realizing how much pain your challenges have put you through in the past, but the process of moving forward is much easier when you know what the problem is and you know what you plan to do about it.

The Plan

1. **State the problem**: First you have to state the real problem that you have been dealing with. This part should be easy now because you identified what the real problem(s) are in your life in Step 4. You are going to do this same process for every problem that you listed in the Courageous Action section of Step 4.

- **Example of my problem:** I never felt true love and a deep connection with my mother or father.

- **Example of my problem:** I didn't think I was worthy of money; therefore, I didn't know how to manage it and thus mismanaged it all the time

2. **State the goal:** Now is the time to put all that you've learned about the SMART method to work. You want to make sure you are tackling the real problem when you write out your goal. You also want to make sure that your goal includes all the items in the SMART method.

- **Example of my goal:** To gain a better understanding of how not feeling loved and having a deep connection with my parents affected my outlook on life by going to therapy for one year.

- **Example of my goal:** To enhance my feelings of worthiness as it pertains to money by learning to save, budget and plan for retirement while taking a money management class by November 30th.

Let's put my goals to the test. I chose two very different goals to show you that any problem can be addressed by setting a goal.

The first problem was an emotional problem. Most people don't think that you can create goals around healing emotional problems, but they are wrong. Emotional problems vary, but a goal will always assist you in the process of dealing with the problem. With emotional problems you should never state absolutes on how you want to feel. For instance I didn't say I wanted to learn to feel loved in six months. That would not be an attainable goal. Who's to say I will ever feel loved, especially in just six months. What this goal does do is give me room to grow.

Now let's take a hard look at this goal: To gain a better understanding of how not feeling loved and having a deep connection with my parents affected my outlook on life by going to therapy for one year. The goal was very **Specific** because I answered the questions of who, what, when, where and why. The who was me, the what was gaining understanding, the when was for the next year, the where was in therapy and the why was so I could feel better about my situation.

The goal was **Measurable** because it would be complete after one year. You must remember that this was an emotional goal, so I had to give myself room to grow. A year may or may not have been enough to accomplish this goal; I was prepared to be flexible with adjusting my timeframe if needed. However, chances were I'd be further along in my understanding of this matter by the time a year went by, so setting my goal for a year really helped me move forward in my life. Even though I had to continue therapy, setting this initial goal was just what I needed to get started.

The goal was also **Attainable** because I knew I was willing to commit to a whole year of therapy. I didn't care how long it took, I just wanted the hurt and the pain I was feeling behind this issue to get resolved. I knew a year of therapy was a good start.

The goal was very **Relevant** to my life. For a long time this problem had been causing all kinds of other problems. It was having a ripple effect and until I understood the major extent of this problem it was going to always cause other problems. Therefore I knew why I was doing this. I was going to therapy to better my future.

Lastly the goal was **Timely** because I knew in a year I could cross this goal off my list. If I needed more time in therapy I would simply create another goal giving myself more time.

Now let's look at the second goal: To enhance my feelings of worthiness as it pertains to money by learning to save, budget and plan for retirement while taking a money management class by November 30th. This goal falls in the category of finances. Most people have financial goals in their life and many of those goals revolve around having or obtaining a specific dollar amount. However, at this time in my life I needed to learn the basics about money. I had started a business and my own personal finances were less than desirable because I was never taught how to manage my money. I made some very detrimental mistakes because I didn't have the proper knowledge. Therefore I needed to go back to the basics and build a firm foundation.

Now let's break this goal down. This goal was **Specific** because again I was able to answer the questions of who, what, when, where and why. The who was me, the what was to learn money management skills, the when was by November 30, the where was in money management class as well as at home and the why was because I wanted to be good at managing my money and I no longer wanted to make costly mistakes that put me and my family in jeopardy.

The goal was **Measurable** because I knew I would have a greater understanding of my finances when the class was complete by November 30th. In addition I knew this goal would be complete after I learned about saving, budgeting and retirement planning because I was very specific when writing out this goal.

This goal was very **Attainable** for me because the class was a set number of weeks and I knew I could do it as long as I committed to attending the class.

This goal was also **Relevant** because I knew that in order to be successful in my personal life and with my business I needed to learn how to manage my money. I was aware that if I understood how to manage my money I could eventually meet some of the financial goals I had swirling around in my head. I knew I would never reach any of my goals without a firm foundation.

Lastly this goal was very **Timely** because I stated that I would complete the class by November 30th. I had already done my research when I wrote this goal by looking into the classes that were available and picking out the one that worked best for me.

Do you see how using the SMART method truly helps you create wonderful goals that address the problem at hand? Now you can begin creating a better future for yourself. Let's put it all together in one final piece.

3. **Write out the entire plan:** When it comes to writing out your plan all you are doing is restating the problem, the goal and the reason why you want to accomplish the goal. Restating the problem is so important because it reminds you of what you are working on when you write out your goal. Restating your goal tells you what you are going to do to correct the problem. Finally writing out why accomplishing this goal is so important to you validates why you have decided to complete the goal in the first place. Having your "why" written in your plan keeps you on track when you want to quit or give up. Here is how I wrote out my plans:

My Plan:

My problem is I never felt true love or a deep connection with my mother or father.

My goal is to gain a better understanding of how not feeling loved or having a deep connection with my parents affected my outlook on life by going to therapy for one year.

I'm doing this because I know having this understanding is going to help me with my relationship with my parents and all my other relationships. I want to be able to have healthy, loving, deeply connected relationships.

My Plan:

My problem is I don't know how to manage my money.

My goal is to enhance my feelings of worthiness as it pertains to money by learning to save, budget and plan for retirement while taking a money management class by November 30th.

I am doing this because I want to become financially successful and the only way to do this is to have a great understanding of how to manage my money. I also want to be able to live a comfortable life and help others financially so I need to learn money management skills.

Now this is how you build a great plan! As you can see it's not very difficult to do. The thing you must concentrate on most is your willingness to see the plan through to the end.

Courageous Action Step:

A. This is a good time to revisit your passion- and purpose-driven questions and your Life List from all the way back in Chapter 2. Reviewing how you answered these questions will help you in determining what goals you want to set for your future.

- Take a look at your Life List. Has anything changed? Are the top things that were important to you when you read Chapter 2 just as important to you now?

- Based on your passion- and purpose-driven questions, your Life List, and any new understandings you may have come to while reading this book, take a shot at writing down in a short phrase what you think your true purpose is. Go with what your gut is telling you and do not second-guess yourself.

Keep your Life List and purpose in mind as you set goals for yourself. Maybe one of your problems is simply that you haven't yet taken the time to do something you really want to do with your life.

B. Now it's your turn to figure out your plan for each of your problems. I want you to begin by answering these questions in your journal. Now that you know and understand the SMART method I want you to apply this method to each one of the questions below and create a goal. Each one of these questions either deals with the real problem you have identified or a category that is going to help enhance your life. When it comes to living out your purpose in life you have to both conquer your challenges and do things to enhance your future.

- What are your real problems? What did you discover in Step 4? (Create a goal around each problem that you want to solve)

- What are your career goals? What do you ultimately want to do and become? (Write out each goal separately)

- What goals do you have for your family? Where would you like to see your family in one to five years? (Write out each goal separately)

- What are your financial goals? What are your plans for saving, budgeting and retirement? (Write out each goal separately)

- What are your spiritual goals? How do you plan to enhance your relationship with God and/or with the world you are a part of? (Write out each goal separately)

- What are your physical or health goals? How do you plan to maintain or obtain a healthy weight? How do you plan to eat better? (Write out each goal separately)

C. Now it's time to write out your plan. This is going to be so great because when you finish you are going to have a roadmap to live by. This plan will guide you into your future and ultimately help you overcome the challenges and problems you have been facing. When you see it all written out you are going to be so proud of yourself.

Now for each goal write out the plan as discussed earlier in this chapter. Make sure you restate the problem and the goal, and be sure to write out why you want to complete the goal.

Example:

My problem is…

My goal is…

I am doing this because…

Choose two of your plans and goals to get started on. These will be the first two that you take action on in the next step.

Courageous Lessons Learned:

Creating a plan with some great goals is the best way to overcome your problems and create a better future for your life. Using the SMART method makes your goals easier to write and more attainable.

CHAPTER 11:
STEP 7 – TAKE ACTION

You made it! You have arrived at the very last section in the Courageous Process and the only way you can truly celebrate is by putting the plan that you just created for your life into action. Everything that you have read in this book is meaningless if you are going to just sit on your hands and do nothing from this point on. If you have followed this book and completed all the exercises that I have given you thus far, you have actually taken a lot of action already and you should be proud of yourself. You have done the work and this should be one of the greatest feelings in the world. But now you have to finish what you started. You just created a plan in the previous section that is going to change your life forever, so you can't quit now.

Let me warn you, this is the part that scares many women off. I'm not sure if it's the word "action" that scares them the most or the thought that action is the one remaining step between them and ultimate success. Whichever it might be, now is the time to push through and complete the work you started. Action is the only way to make big changes in your life and change is what you committed to when you picked this book up and began to read.

How Taking Action Changed My Life

One day I was sitting at my job trying to figure out what was going to make me ultimately happy. I began to play a little game "to quit or not to quit". This was a thought that kept swirling in my head. I knew I was the happiest when I was speaking and that I would love to be able to speak on a more regular basis, but I didn't know how. I had been doing my research about the speaking business and I had gained a lot of knowledge about the industry but I still hadn't decided to make a move. I wanted desperately to leave my current job and start doing my own thing, but I was so scared. What if I failed? What if I didn't make any money? All these questions were legit as there was a definite possibility that those bad things could happen even if I put my all into it.

Then I realized the answer to all my questions, and it hit me like a ton of bricks. I realized that if I never tried I would never know. It was that simple. When that came to me I knew what I had to do. I had been spending so much time trying to figure out if I should quit my job, and now I had my answer. But where should I start?

I want you to remember that I was not independently wealthy; at this point my husband and I were still living paycheck to paycheck. We didn't have a lot of money saved up and I certainly didn't have any money to start a business. This is when I realized the beauty in building a low overhead business. You see, I wanted to become a speaker. I didn't need a building and all the trimmings. All I needed to get started was a computer and a phone so I could interact with women, organizations and companies. Fortunately for me I already had both.

I knew I had what I needed to start a business. Now what was I going to do about money? I couldn't just quit my job without having an alternate plan. Yes, I was about to start a business, but I knew that my business was not going to be able to sustain me right away. I needed to have another plan in place. Then I came up with the perfect idea.

I realized that as a social worker I could get a job doing temporary assignments and still make enough money to survive. In many states contract agencies hire social workers to go into companies or hospitals to do a specific assignment for an allotted amount of time. When the assignment is over the agency tries to find you another assignment. The agency normally pays a higher dollar amount per hour because they don't have to provide benefits to their contractors. This was especially great for me because my husband was willing to carry the family on his insurance benefits. I could work less hours and take home the same amount of money because I was getting paid more as a contractor. I set out to find an agency that had an assignment I could do. Several days later I found one, and I wrote my resignation letter to my employer at the time. I was still taking a risk because I didn't know if the agency would always be able to find work for me, but when it comes to following your dreams you are going to have to take some risks.

I want to stop right here for a minute and make a point. When I was in college I started developing philosophies to live by. These were things I learned that I noticed were true all the time. My first philosophy is one I think you already know and that is *anything is possible*. Another philosophy that rings true in this case is that *there is always a way*. My belief is that no matter how hard a situation might be you can always find a way to solve and get around it. In my case it seemed impossible to quit my job and start my own business. I was also working for one of the most prestigious hospitals in the world, so at the time many people thought I was crazy for wanting to leave a job like that. It's not that I wanted to abandon what I was doing, because as a Medical Social Worker I was actually doing some great work, but I knew God had a bigger calling for me in my life. God wanted to expand my territory and that couldn't happen if I only worked at the hospital.

The day came for me to hand in my resignation letter. To be honest with you I was only a little nervous because I had a plan and I believed in what I was doing. I walked into the Social Work office and I handed my supervisor the letter. She frowned, but it was more of an "I'm sad to see you go but I'm happy you will be able to do what you want" frown than one of anger or disappointment. My department was no stranger to what I wanted to do. They knew I loved speaking and they knew I wanted to do it more than anything. I was always the social worker who tried to motivate everyone, even my fellow co-workers. They were happy and sad at the same time.

Two weeks passed and on my last day the department threw me a going away party. It was so nice and I told everyone that this was not "goodbye" but "see you later" because believe it or not several months later I went back to my same job as a contractor! Now isn't that funny – I got to come back and work less and make the same amount of money. All I can say is God is good!

I officially opened up the doors to Kiki Ramsey International on April 8, 2009. It was such an awesome day! I realized I had done something that I had always wanted to do. I set a goal, took action and actually made it happen! There is no greater feeling than this. To this very day I am still building Kiki Ramsey International. The action never stops.

Where to Start

Now it's your turn. You have this awesome plan and you want to put it into action. The first thing you must do is prioritize. Some people see this as a dirty word but in my opinion prioritizing is what's going to keep you from going insane during this process. You cannot fix all your problems at once. You will drive yourself crazy trying. I coach so many women who set themselves up for failure because they try to be Super Woman and fix everything immediately, forgetting that it took years for them to get in the situation they are currently in. Choose one or two things to work on at the same time so you can succeed.

When you accomplish these two goals then you can pick two more goals to work on.

During the action stage you also have to call on all the courage you have learned throughout reading this book. Taking action calls for you to face some fears, and I get that. This is what I have been preparing you for this whole time. Courage is the act of walking through fear, so in order to reach those goals you've got to put one foot in front of the other and keep on walking.

The day I decided to go after my dream of speaking was one of the best and scariest days of my life. As you are aware I spent a lot of time doing my research. I found out the best places to get started speaking, how to formulate a speech, everything from A to Z. Even though I did my due diligence I had to remember not to spend too much time in the preparation stage because I didn't want to get analysis paralysis and never actually take action.

After I did my research and started making calls, I booked my first speech at a local rotary club, and you know how the rest of the story goes. Since that time I have spoken before thousands of women all around the world on how to transform their life and career. The moral of the story is none of this would have happened in my life had I not taken the first step and gotten up in front of that tiny rotary club audience. That action changed my life.

What is your first step? You bought this book because you wanted me to help you overcome your fear so you could walk in your purpose. Well, here is your chance, the moment you have been waiting for. This is your time to step out there and get courageous. Taking this next step will change your life. You have been through a series of steps and processes to prepare you for this moment. You are ready. The action that you take now will set you on your own path of discovery. If you decide to stick it out then you are truly headed on a path to a courageous life, a life that you have only dreamed of, a life of your design.

Courageous Action Step:

Look back on the plans that you wrote down during the Courageous Action from the previous chapter. Now you should choose two of your plans and work on those.

Choose the ones that mean the most to you right now. No one can tell you what to choose. Call attention to the plans you choose with some kind of marking, like a special symbol or with a highlighter.

Now that you have made your choice I want you to think of the very first thing you can do to get started on each of the two plans. Set aside a place in your journal, or another place that you see every day, to write these steps down.

Here comes the scary part. Take a deep breath. Are you ready? Do it! As soon as you possibly can, take the first steps towards your two goals. This is where most people fail. It doesn't matter how hard or easy the problem you choose to work on is if you don't do anything about it. Without taking action you will never see progress. Once you have finished these steps, check them off wherever you wrote them down. Then plan what to do next – and do it. Check that off when complete. Repeat until you have reached your goal.

This is how you do it. You are now doing what you set out to do from page one. Are you proud of yourself? You definitely should be!

Courageous Lessons Learned:

Once you have made a plan for your life, all that's left to achieve your goal is to take action. Stick to your plan and go for it! You can't do everything at once, so remember to prioritize your goals and work on them a few at a time.

PART III:

COMMITTING TO COURAGE

Congratulations, you are now ready to live in your purpose! I am so happy I could walk with you throughout this process. It has been a pleasure and a real honor to be allowed on this journey with you. My prayer is that God continues to bless your life and that you live out your purpose and courage each day!

Don't be intimidated by the fact that this book has a Part III – this section is here for your benefit, to help you keep the commitment to the promise you have made to yourself and the plans you have put together to achieve your goals. In this last section you will learn to stop making excuses that hold you back from your dreams, and you will have the opportunity to practice living in courage with a special week-long exercise.

You have pumped up your courage muscle and set your sights on your purpose, and you put in a lot of hard work to get to this point. It's vital that you don't quit now or ever again!

CHAPTER 12:
NO MORE EXCUSES

You have made it through what has been one of your life's most challenging but most rewarding processes, but there is still one thing that can stand in your way of success: excuses. One of my biggest pet peeves is all the excuses we allow ourselves to accept about our circumstances. If something is hard, we give ourselves a reason not to do it. We have gotten so used to doing this that we disguise these excuses as reasons because we think if we have a valid reason not to do something, then it's ok not to do it. The truth is fear shows up as excuses, which are just bad reasons to let ourselves off the hook from doing things that scare us but are important to our overall success. To move forward, complete your plan, and overcome the issues that have been causing you so much pain, you must accept that you will be scared, and excuses are not the answer.

I want you to examine yourself. Have you noticed that you are scared deep down when you give yourself an excuse not to do something? I know this is hard to admit, and you may not have realized that you did it. Any time I find myself fighting hard against doing something, I realize I am scared. If you admit this is also true for you, don't feel bad; it's a normal reaction. You have to learn to recognize it and stop it when it happens. People find excuses for anything when it comes to neglecting to take action in your life. For example, you can easily find an excuse for staying in a job you are unhappy with.

You might tell yourself you must stay until you get enough retirement saved, the job pays too much money to quit, or my favorite - you have too many years invested, and now you can't quit. These are excuses that you allow to keep you in an unhealthy place in your life. How long are you willing to sacrifice your ultimate happiness for something that only makes you feel better temporarily? People do it every day, which is why so many people are unhappy. They are choosing not to change their circumstances because they somehow have justified their unhappiness in their own minds.

Here are some examples of excuses you might have given yourself not to follow your dreams. These are also some of the excuses I used to give myself.

1. I don't have enough time.
2. I am just not good enough to do what I want to do.
3. I do not know how to do what I'm trying to do.
4. I don't know enough to do what I want to do.
5. I don't know what I want.
6. I don't know my purpose.
7. I'm too tired by the end of the day to work on other stuff.
8. There are not enough hours in the day for me to get it all done.
9. It's just too hard.
10. I'm always too tired.
11. My full-time job is holding me back.
12. The children require too much time.
13. I'm too old to go back to school.
14. I will never be successful because success is for other people.
15. I will never make it because I don't have enough money.
16. No one wants to buy what I have because I just got started.

17. I am not motivated to complete the tasks I need to do.

18. I don't have enough money to do everything I need to do for my business.

19. I don't have enough help to do everything I need to do.

20. I have to work to make money because my own business is not making money; therefore, I don't have enough time to devote to my own business.

21. I don't want to fail, so I need to do more research.

22. I'm not creative, so I need to look at what everyone else is doing.

23. I can't teach or talk about money because I am poor and don't have any.

24. No one will listen to me because I'm not good enough.

25. No one supports my dreams.

26. Other people are judging me, so I won't try.

27. I can't go to that meeting because someone will judge the car I'm driving.

28. I just don't have time to exercise.

29. I can't go to that seminar or get coaching even though it might change my life because I don't have time, need a babysitter, need to sleep, or can't afford it.

Have I given you enough excuses to think about? The last one is the one that makes me the saddest. I see many women forgo potentially life-changing experiences for their excuses. But what I have learned is we women make time for the things we value. So, no more excuses. It's time to overcome your fears and place value on the things that can change your life.

Another big excuse I often hear is number 28: I don't have time to exercise. Once again, we make time for what is important to us. If you truly want to commit to a healthy lifestyle and exercise is a part of that plan, you will find some way to fit it into your schedule, even if you start gradually.

Now, if you truly don't want to do something, that's ok. Just admit that it is not in your plans at the moment, be ok with your decision, and move on. At the end of the day, we all have a choice to make about how we spend our time. We all have the same twenty-four hours in a day. Choosing not to do something because it doesn't fit your plan and making an excuse about not doing it are two different things. When you make a choice, you are owning your power. When you make an excuse, you are not accepting that you have a choice, and you give your power away.

Breaking Out of the Blame Game

As you may recall, I used to blame my mother for everything. When I got pregnant at sixteen years old, I blamed her for not being a good mother and making sure I had all the knowledge I needed about sex. I blamed her for giving me a terrible childhood because she was on drugs. From my misery and unhappiness to my temper to my inability to love in a healthy way – when I say I blamed her for everything, I mean it. However, blaming my mother did not help my situation. It was only hurting me further. I didn't realize it at the time, but using my mother as my scapegoat was pushing me further and further away from my purpose. For me to become the person I am today, I had to embrace the fact that God put me in those specific circumstances to grow me as a person. I needed to embrace the challenge and learn how to navigate my way through so God could show me exactly what He made me for. It took me years to overcome what I went through with my mother, and it didn't happen until I stopped blaming her for my unhappiness and realized that she was not the cause of everything. I realized that I had been giving my power away for years when I could have accepted responsibility and made different choices to improve my life.

When I realized my mother wasn't to blame for my misfortunes, I had to change my tune. I had to suck it up, dry my tears, and commit to moving forward, excuses and blame-free. This was one of the most freeing experiences I ever had. Through this process, I gained back my freedom and power to choose. Before this moment, all my excuses held me hostage from the progress I wanted to make in my life because that's what excuses do; they hold you back from discovering the life you deserve. If you are anything like I was, and your excuses hold you hostage from the life you want to pursue, it's time to let them go.

No excuse is more important than stepping up and living out your purpose in life. Nothing should keep you from the happiness God has for you. No matter how scared you are, you have to take a risk and bet on yourself. Trust and believe you can beat the odds no matter how much they are stacked against you. From this day forward, commit to living your life without excuses.

Accept the Risk

Everyone who embraces a life without excuses must also accept the risk that comes with this lifestyle. This means when something terrible happens, and I do mean when and not if, you have to push forward, accept that this is your life, and assume full responsibility. You have to accept that risks are a part of the game. The saying is true: low risk, low reward; big risk, big reward. Ask yourself what type of life you are looking for. Do you want to live a life where you experience everything you ever imagined? Where you get to share wonderful experiences with your family, have the career of your dreams, live in the house you want, and even drive the type of car you want? If the answer is yes, it's time to take some chances and step out of your comfort zone. Accept the risk that things will not be easy, but it will be worth it.

Eliminating the Self-Limiter

The self-limiter is that voice inside of you that tells you that you can't do something and are not confident enough. We have all heard it occasionally, and it is the ultimate discouragement in our lives. This is your negative voice, the part of your inner self that always sees the glass as half-empty.

We all have two voices inside of us, one that cheers us on and one that tries to knock us down (which is the self-limiter). The sad part is most people listen to the self-limiter and not the other helpful voice when it comes to important things in life. Most people fall into the trap of looking at the worst possible outcome of a situation before they even explore the good that could happen. Does any of this sound like you? Listen, I have been there, done that. I got so bad that I would look at a specific situation in my life and automatically think the worst would happen. My self-limiter would say, "There is no way you will get that job. The salary is too high, and the responsibilities are too much for you to handle." Then, I would go into the interview with a less-than-enthusiastic attitude because I had already defeated myself. My self-limiter had already won. You know it's bad when the job was actually perfect for you, and you talked yourself right out of it because you chose to believe the negative. It happens every day, and it has to stop if you are going to make your dreams come true.

Courageous Action Step:

1. Looking back at your journal entries from Steps 6 and 7, choose one of the two most important goals you have decided to act on. Write out your goal in a clean space in your journal.

2. Now, on that same page, write the word "excuses" at the top underneath your goal.

3. Under the word "excuses," I want you to write out every excuse you have ever made for why you cannot reach the goal you wrote down. You might have ten, twenty, or more excuses. The number doesn't matter because this is your chance to get it all out and be completely honest about what excuses have held you back.

4. Now, next to each excuse, I want you to write one reason why you can reach this goal. That's right, if you have ten excuses, you need to write ten reasons why you can succeed. So if one of your excuses was, "I can't reach my dream because I don't have enough money," you could write that you can make all the money you need to follow your dream. Or if you said, "I am just not good enough to accomplish what I want to accomplish," your reason why you are good enough is you are smart, and you can figure out anything you want to figure out.

5. Once you are done, I want you to circle your top three reasons why you can accomplish your goal. This is what I call your Top 3 Reasons to Succeed! These are the answers to your excuses and your self-limiter. These three reasons can motivate you during hard times and give you more confidence when you are up.

6. Write these three reasons on a separate piece of paper and keep them with you at all times.

7. You can repeat this process as many times as you need for any other goals whenever you are ready to take action.

Now, how cool is this? You might have been giving yourself every reason to fail and not try hard enough for so long, but now that's over. Whenever you think negatively about accomplishing your dreams, goals, or passions, you can pull out your Top 3 Reasons to Succeed and remind yourself that there are no excuses not to succeed.

This exercise will truly keep you on track when you find it hard to keep going. You are learning strategies to keep fear in its place, and I commend you for coming this far. I know I have said this before, but most people's fear stops them way before they get to this point. As you have learned throughout this book, it takes work to step out of your comfort zone and do the work necessary to change your life. But you, my friend, are different – you will make it.

Courageous Lessons Learned:

Your excuses and self-limiter will keep you stuck in a rut that is difficult to get out of. However, if you stop giving yourself excuses and shut your self-limiter up, you can reach any dream you want.

CHAPTER 13:
CHASING PURPOSE AND FINDING HAPPINESS

Before we jump into the final step of this book, the 7-Day Courageous Challenge, I would be remiss if I didn't bring it all together and share how pursuing a life filled with purpose leads to a life full of joy and happiness. As I was revising this book, I knew this piece needed to be added.

Since I was that 10-year-old girl sleeping on that couch in that crack house, I have been on a mission to find purpose and happiness. However, I didn't know how the two were so intertwined. Since this book's first edition, I have returned to school and gotten two additional degrees—a Master's in Positive Psychology Coaching and a PhD in Business Psychology. Needless to say, I have committed my career to the study of happiness and strengths. Throughout all my research and life experiences, I have learned that happiness does not exist without purpose. What do I mean by this? Well, happiness, in its truest form, is not just a fleeting emotion but a sustained state of being that arises when we align with our purpose. Therefore, the question becomes, what is happiness? Happiness is that inner glow, those positive emotions, and the contentment that comes from knowing you are on the right path, living a life of passion and purpose. I believe purpose is God's hand guiding us through life's journey, and happiness naturally follows when our actions align with our deeper meaning. The mere fact that you decided to discover and follow your purpose can result in a happy life.

I didn't realize that when I started helping my mom get off of drugs all those years ago, it would lead to a life filled with purpose where I could pour into and coach women all over the world with my words. I would say back then, I was the absolute opposite of happy. I was miserable. I was sad. I was angry. I was hurt. That's the funny thing about purpose and happiness. Our purpose is often born out of a lot of pain and hurt, and being courageous enough to find a solution becomes the very thing that you were placed on this earth for and the thing that makes you the happiest in life. But many of us struggle with finding true happiness because we are chasing success.

Purpose, Happiness, and Success

Don't get me wrong; I have always wanted to be successful, and I'm sure the same is true for you if you're reading this book. I mean, for goodness sake, I promised myself at ten years old that no matter what bad things happened in my life, I would be successful. I meant every word when I made that promise, and I owe much of my accomplishments to that promise. However, there was a point in my life when only success mattered, and I thought I could get it without walking in my purpose. I began chasing success so much that I jeopardized my family's financial health more than I care to admit. What I am saying is I made some terrible mistakes all in the name of chasing success, and it caused a lot of pain and damage to my family. This time in my life was one of my lowest because I thought I knew better. I had come so far and learned many lessons, but the chase for success took me away from God's will for my life. But I serve an amazing God who has given me an amazing, godly husband who was always there to remind me who I was and my purpose in life. I am so grateful I got back on track and finally learned that success does not make us happy. It's the pursuit of purpose that ultimately makes you happy, and then success follows.

You see, the pursuit of success only leaves you chasing success. And when you reach a level of success, it never satisfies you like you thought, and you start all over chasing a higher success. Psychologists call this the Hedonic treadmill, which states that your happiness level will always return to the state it was before a positive or negative experience. In other words, after reaching a level of success, you will inevitably feel the same way you felt before you reached that level. This is why you see so many successful women who are never satisfied with their success, no matter how successful they are. I didn't want this for myself and I certainly don't want this life for you. So what do you do? Do you stop chasing success? Do you change who you are and give up all your ambitions? Certainly not. I have not given up my ambitions and drive. As a matter of fact, I am more driven than I was in my earlier life because I shifted my focus. Now, I only chase purpose and practice gratitude. When you chase purpose and practice gratitude, happiness, and success will follow.

Chasing Purpose

You see, the minute I turned my focus back to my God-given purpose of helping women create their own happiness and transform their lives and careers, God began to bless me immensely. The struggle for financial gain began to dissipate. My words of encouragement were more powerful, and I have been able to help more women than I could have ever imagined. And it's all because I stopped chasing success and placed my focus on helping people. God has placed each of us on this earth to help someone else. This is your overarching purpose in life. The beautiful thing is that God gives us favor and allows us to figure out how we will help other people. I call this the vehicle. You get to choose from a million different ways to help others. Therefore, your goal in life is to find the way that best suits you and begin pursuing it. And when you do, doors that you thought were closed or would never become available to you start to open. This is all because you chose to chase purpose and not success.

I know this concept can be hard to grasp. It was hard for me to grasp at first as well. It feels like you are letting go of your future. Like you no longer have control over your destiny. The opposite is the truth. When you choose to focus on your purpose, you are actually taking control of the destiny God already has planned for you. When you chase purpose, anything is possible in your life.

Practicing Gratitude

Practicing gratitude has served as the cornerstone in seamlessly integrating purpose into the fabric of my everyday life. Just as I shifted my focus from the relentless pursuit of success to the meaningful pursuit of helping others, incorporating gratitude into my daily routine allowed me to fully appreciate the blessings that came with aligning myself with my God-given purpose. Gratitude is a constant reminder of the abundant gifts and opportunities that surround us, even amid challenges. It is a powerful force that transforms ordinary moments into extraordinary ones, fostering a sense of contentment and fulfillment. As I express gratitude for the ability to impact the lives of women seeking happiness and transformation, I find myself even more deeply connected to my overarching purpose. Acknowledging and appreciating the goodness in my life amplifies the impact of my efforts, making the journey toward purpose not only fulfilling but enriching in ways I could not have anticipated. In essence, gratitude becomes the catalyst for a harmonious blend of purpose-driven living and a continuous cycle of blessings as I am reminded each day of the significance of my chosen path. Just as chasing purpose opened doors I never thought possible, practicing gratitude has illuminated the path, making the journey purposeful and profoundly gratifying.

For women, the practice of gratitude takes on a particularly empowering and transformative role in our lives. In the pursuit of purpose, we often face unique challenges and societal expectations. Embracing gratitude becomes a tool for navigating these complexities, providing a sanctuary of strength and resilience. Cultivating gratitude allows women to walk in our purpose unapologetically and acknowledge and celebrate our achievements, no matter how small, fostering a positive self-image and reinforcing the idea that our contributions are valuable.

I have learned that gratitude becomes a means of reclaiming agency over our narrative in a world where women encounter so many disparities and inequalities. By expressing gratitude for our strengths, passions, and the ability to make a difference, we are empowered to overcome obstacles and defy societal constraints. I love gratitude because it becomes a form of self-love, encouraging us to appreciate our worth and the significance of the world with our purpose.

Simply put, the practice of gratitude in the pursuit of purpose creates a ripple effect in your life, allowing you to share your purpose with the world, thus creating a life full of contribution, happiness, and success.

Committing to a Purpose-Driven Life

Committing to a purpose-driven life is like embarking on a transformative journey where the pursuit of success takes a back seat, and the desire to make a meaningful impact becomes the driving force. Drawing inspiration from my own experience of redirecting my focus toward helping women transform their lives and careers, I realized that committing to a purpose-driven life was synonymous with unlocking a cascade of blessings. By giving up the focus on financial gain and success and redirecting my energy towards uplifting others, the resonance of my words of encouragement became more profound, and my capacity to make a difference expanded beyond my imagination.

In committing to a purpose-driven life, you will discover a profound sense of alignment with your true self and a purpose larger than personal success. This journey, which calls you to be dedicated to serving others, offers a deep and lasting fulfillment that transcends any material achievements.

As you commit to a purpose-driven life, you will find a profound clarity of vision, allowing you to discern the significance of your role in the greater narrative of life. The pursuit of personal success often comes with the pressure of societal expectations and external validations. In contrast, the commitment to purpose empowers you to define your own measure of success based on your positive impact on others. This transformative journey opens up avenues of empathy, compassion, and understanding, fostering a harmonious connection with the world around you.

Moreover, committing to a purpose-driven life leads to discovering resilience and strength within. The challenges encountered on this path become opportunities for growth, learning, and refining your purpose. It is through adversity that the true depth of your commitment is tested, revealing the strength that arises from a genuine desire to contribute positively to the well-being of others.

In essence, committing to a purpose-driven life is a journey of self-discovery, compassion, and empowerment. It is a realization that success, as conventionally defined, pales in comparison to the profound satisfaction derived from knowing that your existence is purposeful and that you are an integral part of a collective journey towards a better, more harmonious world. Here's to your purpose-driven life.

Courageous Action Step:

Decide that you are going to start living a purpose-driven life. In your journal, write out what your purpose-driven life looks like, begin following this vision daily, and watch how happy and successful you will become.

Courageous Lesson Learned:

The pursuit of success alone only leaves you chasing a never-ending and unfulfilling existence. But the pursuit of purpose will bring you all the happiness and success your heart can handle.

CHAPTER 14:
THE 7 DAY COURAGEOUS CHALLENGE

This last chapter is all about you. I understand how hard it is to get started and I just want to give you a little boost. You have decided not to allow fear and excuses to hold you back anymore. Over the next seven days you will be challenged to take a real stand against your fears.

This challenge is designed to help you *jumpstart* your courageousness. I stress the word "jumpstart" because courage is a habit that you must feed daily, weekly, monthly, and yearly for a lifetime. The more you strengthen it, the better it will serve you.

If you let it, the Courageous Challenge can set you on your way. It is designed to be started on any day of the week, any time of the month or year. What matters most is your effort. You will get out of the experience as much as you put into it.

I recommend that you commit to doing each daily challenge and give at least 10-15 minutes for the daily reflection. You can continue to use your journal for any reflective writing you would like to do. Trust me, a little fearless action followed by just 10-15 minutes of honest reflection will make a huge differ-ence in your attitude, gratitude, energy, your day and your life.

Now let's go!

DAY ONE: FACE YOURSELF

Daily Challenge

To know yourself is one of the greatest gifts you can give yourself and those you love. Begin this journey by taking some time to think and record your thoughts on these questions:

- What do you want out of your life? Forget what you've always been told you should want and consider the truth of what would actually make you happy. Why aren't you living that truth?

- What are you afraid of? Mentally, emotionally, financially, socially...what things produce fear in you?

- What are your personality flaws? Do you give up easily? Will you bully or manipulate to get what you want? Do you struggle to be honest with loved ones? Do you allow your self-limiter to get in your way of success?

Reflection

You spent Day One reflecting on who you are, what you want, and what you fear. How did that experience make you feel? Did your assessment leave you encouraged, sad, resolved, or something else? What can you do with the knowledge and insights you gained from today?

As you reflect, remember that we are all flawed. We all struggle to be the highest versions of ourselves and all fall short at times. So don't let any of this get you down. Let it be a catalyst.

Also, be encouraged by the knowledge that you've done something very courageous. It takes great courage to look honestly at your life – both the good and bad. That is the reason many go through life with blinders on; it's easier that way. But courage rarely comes from doing what is easy.

DAY TWO: DO SOMETHING THAT SCARES YOU

Daily Challenge

As babies, we are fearless. We take that first step, say that first word, and pick up unfamiliar things with little regard for consequence. We have infinite courage that, over time, is either reinforced or stripped away by life events.

Today, recapture some of that fearlessness by doing something that scares you. This can include things like:

- Starting a conversation with a stranger
- Asking someone out or telling someone you love them
- Asking for a promotion
- Being truly vulnerable, open, honest and transparent with someone you love
- Volunteering to speak in public
- Leaving a comfortable situation for the unknown

Choose something that frightens you or that you would otherwise avoid, but not something that could put you at risk or cause harm to you or another.

Reflection

What did you choose and why? Today, you looked into the eyes of fear and forced it to retreat. It was a great step toward cultivating a spirit of confidence. Reflect now on what you did and how it made you feel. Are you able to see the value in your efforts, even if the outcome wasn't what you wanted? Did it make you feel stronger or more fearful?

Courage is not the absence of fear. Courage is moving ahead in spite of fear, to go on living, dreaming and trying. Hopefully, you'll keep doing what scares you long after today.

DAY THREE: DO SOMETHING NEW

Daily Challenge

We don't grow or learn from doing the same things all of the time. So today, do or try something you've never experienced before. This can include things as simple as:

- Taking a different route home
- Having something new for lunch or dinner
- Taking a dance or yoga class
- Trying a new machine at the gym
- Picking a book to read that you normally wouldn't

What you pick doesn't have to be drastic or costly as long as it will give you a chance to be exposed to new things, people, or places.

Reflection

What did you choose and why? Some people believe that the older you get, the more you know. That's mostly true, but it's never an excuse to stop learning or experiencing. Was it hard for you to come up with something new to do today? Why do you think that is?

Did you enjoy what you did? Did it make you nervous? Excited? Rejuvenated? What other things would you like to try? Make a list and set about regularly scheduling new experiences into your life.

DAY FOUR: DO SOMETHING FOR SOMEONE ELSE

Daily Challenge

There is courage in forging our own paths, but also in being willing to sacrifice on behalf of others. Use today to give a bit of your time for someone else.

Think of someone in your life or a stranger that you can do something nice or helpful for today. It could be as simple as:

- Picking up dinner for a sick friend
- Grabbing coffee for a busy coworker
- Visiting with an elderly neighbor
- Volunteering at a community-based charity
- Helping a homeless person out

Again, your effort doesn't need to be costly or drastic. It's also not necessary for the other person to be aware of your act of kindness.

Reflection

What did you choose to do and why? We can easily fall into the trap of only seeing soldiers and firefighters as being courageous. Why do you think it's courageous for everyday people to do something for someone else? What sacrifice did you have to make for the other person and how did it make you feel?

DAY FIVE: CREATE SOMETHING

Daily Challenge

It takes courage to put your time and energy into creating something. As children, we overflow with creative energy and ingenuity. Over time, we become disconnected from that part of ourselves.

For today's challenge, take some time to create something.

- Draw a picture.
- Write a poem or short story.
- Sew or knit something.
- Decorate a floral arrangement.
- Do a home improvement project.

Don't think about it too much or agonize over it. Just do it. Put your focus into letting your mind drift and flow as it will. Don't judge, don't edit, don't second guess. Just create.

Reflection

What did you choose to create and why? What did it feel like to create without censoring yourself? Was it harder or easier than expected? What if you had to share what you created with a friend? What about a complete stranger? Could you do it?

Don't be fooled; to be creative is to be courageous. You are, in essence, putting a bit of yourself into whatever you make, write, etc., and there is always a level of fear that it will be harshly judged. But to create is part of what we are here to do. When you suppress that, you've suppressed a part of your being.

DAY SIX: COMMIT TO ENDING SOMETHING

Daily Challenge

Just as we can get into ruts and fail to try or experience new things, it's also easy for us to cling to behaviors, things, and thoughts that are no longer serving us well. Today, you are challenged to put an end to that. Today is the day you commit to and act on ending something. This can include:

- Stopping the negative self-talk and negative thinking. When your thoughts float to believing something negative about yourself, commit to changing it to a positive statement.

- Not spending money on things you don't need (i.e., buying lunch daily, unnecessary shopping, coffee, etc.).

- Letting go of an unhealthy relationship. You might try writing a letter, sending an email or calling the person on the phone, explaining why you need to distance yourself.

Reflection

What did you choose to end and why? Have you ever gone for any length of time without that behavior, thing or person, i.e., have you ever gone a day without beating yourself up with your negative self-talk or thoughts? Or have you ever really tried to put an end to this unhealthy relationship?

What scares you about ending your particular "thing" (i.e., are you afraid to believe that amazing things can happen in your life, or are you scared to be alone and experience the unknown)? What steps can you take to help you through any hard times in your effort to eliminate this behavior, thing, person or way of thinking from your life? Are there people who will support or undermine you? How will you handle them?

DAY SEVEN: COMMIT TO BEGINNING SOMETHING

Daily Challenge

Yesterday, I challenged you to end something that was no longer serving you. The great thing about endings is that they leave the door open for new beginnings.

Today, start something new and positive for yourself. You could:

- Commit to saving more money (for example, you could put the money saved by not buying lunch everyday into your savings account).

- Commit to a new phase in a key relationship by sitting down for an honest conversation, going on a date, or playing a game and spending quality time with your kids.

- Start a new love relationship with your body by buying a new bathing suit or new lingerie, or going to the gym and eating healthy.

As with yesterday, you need to commit not only in your head, but with an action. The action is what gives you momentum. But be honest and only commit to something you really want.

Reflection

What did you choose to begin and why? Take some time to reflect on today's challenge and the entire week.

What things have you learned about yourself today and throughout the week? Are you encouraged and motivated? If not, why? What do you think may be holding you back?

Are you ready to begin a new phase in your life? Do you have a better vision for what you want that phase to look like? What specific efforts will you make to keep your momentum going? Do you feel like you challenged yourself to step out of your comfort zone?

Guess what?

You made it through the week! You made it through the challenge!

Give yourself a pat on the back, a round of applause, or a big, big hug. You deserve it!

Courage, like many things, is learned. We naturally have a certain amount of it at birth, but tend to lose our connection with it over time. Or we start to draw courage from false sources – like money or appearance. Neither of those things matter.

Courage is our right. It is ours to embrace and use regardless of how we look, what we have, or where we live. It is not derived from anything external.

Throughout the week, we may have used some external motivations or experiences to help bring out our inner lionesses, but it was WHAT'S IN YOU – bestowed upon you at birth – that drove you to tap into that deep well of fearlessness and act. So yeah! You go girl!

Now, I beg you not to stop. Build momentum and become the YOU of your dreams. **PRACTICE** the art of being courageous and living courageously. **CHOOSE** to see failures as learning and growing opportunities and not get stuck in negativity. **SPEAK** supportive words to your spirit and find the strength to go on when times get hard. **SURROUND** yourself with people who love you and want to see you walk fully in your courage and purpose.

It's Your Time to Get Courageous Now!

CONCLUSION

Wow! You have worked through a lot of steps in this book to help you truly discover your passions and purpose in life. You've probably cried, screamed, laughed, and maybe even jumped for joy while reading this book. But my biggest hope is that you've grown from what you have learned.

The only real way to change your life is to acquire new knowledge and to grow from it. It took me a long time to learn the knowledge that I put in this book. Don't beat yourself up if some of the steps were difficult to accomplish. Growth takes time, and no one grows to his or her full potential overnight. I can remember working through all the steps, thinking that I would never come to a place where I felt good about my life. But I was wrong. I actually came to a place where I felt amazing about my life, and now I'm able to help other women like you feel amazing about their lives, too. It just may take a little time.

Use this book as a guide for your life. Read it over and over again until things get easier and better. It's never too late to get your breakthrough. It's never too late to live the passionate and purposeful life God wants for you.

My biggest goal in life is for others to see God through me and the work I do. I don't do this work for myself. I don't stay up working late and losing sleep just so I can serve myself. No, this is an assignment that God has given me, and I vowed when my mother passed away to commit my life to God's work. That's exactly what he wants from you too. He wants you to be his hands and his feet on earth. The truth is someone else's life is depending on you discovering and fulfilling your purpose. You were placed here for a reason, and I hope Get Courageous Now has helped you get closer to that purpose.

Thank you from the bottom of my heart for allowing me to be on this journey called life with you. It means so much to me that you trusted me with the most intimate and challenging details of your life. My prayers are that you go out and change the world with your gifts and talents. I would love to hear how this book has helped you. What changes have you made, and what strategies and steps have helped you most? I invite you to connect with me on social media and share your story with me. You never know. Your success story might just be in my next book.

Please don't stop on your journey here. Build momentum and become the YOU of your dreams. PRACTICE the art of being courageous and living courageously. CHOOSE to see failures as learning and growing opportunities and not to get stuck in negativity. SPEAK supportive words to your spirit and find the strength to go on when times get hard. SURROUND yourself with people who love you and want you to want to see you walk fully in your courage and purpose.

It's your Time To Get Courageous Now.

Your friend and coach,

Dr. Kiki Ramsey